LIGUORI CATHOLIC BIBLE STUDY

Wisdom Books

JOB, PSALMS, PROVERBS, ECCLESIASTES, SONG OF SONGS, WISDOM, SIRACH (BEN SIRA)

WILLIAM A. ANDERSON, DMIN, PHD

Liguori
LIGUORI, MISSOURI

Imprimi Potest:
Harry Grile, CSsR, Provincial
Denver Province, The Redemptorists

Printed with Ecclesiastical Permission and Approved for Private or Instructional Use

Nihil Obstat: Rev. Msgr. Kevin Michael Quirk, JCD, JV
　　　　　Censor Librorum

Imprimatur: + Michael J. Bransfield
　　　　　Bishop of Wheeling-Charleston [West Virginia]
　　　　　March 17, 2014

Published by Liguori Publications
Liguori, Missouri 63057

To order, visit Liguori.org or call 800-325-9521.

Library of Congress Cataloging-in-Publication Data
Anderson, William Angor, 1937-
　Wisdom books : Job, Psalms, Proverbs, Ecclesiastes, Song of Songs, Wisdom, Sirach /
William A. Anderson, DMin, PhD.—First Edition.
　　pages cm.—(Liguori Catholic Bible study)
　ISBN 978-0-7648-2139-4
1. Wisdom literature—Study and teaching. I. Title.
　BS1456.A53 2014
　223.0071—dc23
　　　　　　　　2014018793

p ISBN 978-0-7648-2139-4
e ISBN 978-0-7648-6985-3

Liguori Publications, a nonprofit corporation, is an apostolate of The Redemptorists. To learn more about The Redemptorists, visit Redemptorists.com.

Printed in the United States of America
18 17 16 15 14 / 5 4 3 2 1
First Edition

Contents

NOTE: The length of each Bible section varies. Group leaders should combine sections as needed to fit the number of sessions in their program.

Dedication

THIS SERIES is lovingly dedicated to the memory of my parents, Angor and Kathleen Anderson, in gratitude for all they shared with all who knew them, especially my siblings and me.

Acknowledgments

BIBLE STUDIES and reflections depend on the help of others who read the manuscript and make suggestions. I am especially indebted to Sister Anne Francis Bartus, CSJ, DMin, whose vast experience and knowledge were very helpful in bringing this series to its final form.

Introduction to
Liguori Catholic Bible Study

READING THE BIBLE can be daunting. It's a complex book, and many a person of goodwill has tried to read the Bible and ended up putting it down in utter confusion. It helps to have a companion, and *Liguori Catholic Bible Study* is a solid one. Over the course of this series, you'll learn about biblical messages, themes, personalities, and events and understand how the books of the Bible rose out of the need to address new situations.

Across the centuries, people of faith have asked, "Where is God in this moment?" Millions of Catholics look to the Bible for encouragement in their journey of faith. Wisdom teaches us not to undertake Bible study alone, disconnected from the Church that was given Scripture to share and treasure. When used as a source of prayer and thoughtful reflection, the Bible comes alive.

Your choice of a Bible-study program should be dictated by what you want to get out of it. One goal of *Liguori Catholic Bible Study* is to give readers greater familiarity with the Bible's structure, themes, personalities, and message. But that's not enough. This program will also teach you to use Scripture in your prayer. God's message is as compelling and urgent today as ever, but we get only part of the message when it's memorized and stuck in our head. It's meant for the entire person—physical, emotional, and spiritual.

We're baptized into life with Christ, and we're called to live more fully with Christ today as we practice the values of justice, peace, forgiveness, and community. God's new covenant was written on the hearts of the people of Israel; we, their spiritual descendants, are loved that intimately by God today. *Liguori Catholic Bible Study* will draw you closer to God, in whose image and likeness we are fashioned.

Group and Individual Study

The *Liguori Catholic Bible Study* series is intended for group and individual study and prayer. This series gives you the tools to start a study group. Gathering two or three people in a home or announcing the meeting of a Bible-study group in a parish or community can bring surprising results. Each lesson in this series contains a section to help groups study, reflect, pray, and share biblical reflections. Each lesson but the first also has a second section for individual study.

Many people who want to learn more about the Bible don't know where to begin. This series gives them a place to start and helps them continue until they're familiar with all the books of the Bible.

Bible study can be a lifelong project, always enriching those who wish to be faithful to God's Word. When people complete a study of the whole Bible, they can begin again, making new discoveries with each new adventure into the Word of God.

Lectio Divina
(Sacred Reading)

BIBLE STUDY isn't just a matter of gaining intellectual knowledge of the Bible; it's also about gaining a greater understanding of God's love and concern for creation. The purpose of reading and knowing the Bible is to enrich our relationship with God. God loves us and gave us the Bible to illustrate that love. In his April 12, 2013, address before the Pontifical Biblical Commission, Pope Francis stressed that "the Church's life and mission are founded on the Word of God which is the soul of theology and at the same time inspires the whole of Christian life."

The Meaning of *Lectio Divina*

Lectio divina is a Latin expression that means "divine or sacred reading." The process for *lectio divina* consists of Scripture readings, reflection, and prayer. Many clergy, religious, and laity use *lectio divina* in their daily spiritual reading to develop a closer and more loving relationship with God. Learning about Scripture has as its purpose the living of its message, which demands a period of reflection on Scripture passages.

Prayer and *Lectio Divina*

Prayer is a necessary element for the practice of *lectio divina*. The entire process of reading and reflecting is a prayer. It's not merely an intellectual pursuit; it's also a spiritual one. Page 15 includes an Opening Prayer for gathering one's thoughts before moving on to the passages in each section.

This prayer may be used privately or in a group. For those who use the book for daily spiritual reading, the prayer for each section may be repeated each day. Some may wish to keep a journal of each day's meditation.

Pondering the Word of God

Lectio divina is the ancient Christian spiritual practice of reading the holy Scriptures with intentionality and devotion. This practice helps Christians center themselves and descend to the level of the heart to enter an inner quiet space, finding God.

This sacred reading is distinct from reading for knowledge or information, and it's more than the pious practice of spiritual reading. It is the practice of opening ourselves to the action and inspiration of the Holy Spirit. As we intentionally focus on and become present to the inner meaning of the Scripture passage, the Holy Spirit enlightens our minds and hearts. We come to the text willing to be influenced by a deeper meaning that lies within the words and thoughts we ponder.

In this space, we open ourselves to be challenged and changed by the inner meaning we experience. We approach the text in a spirit of faith and obedience as a disciple ready to be taught by the Holy Spirit. As we savor the sacred text, we let go of our usual control of how we expect God to act in our lives and surrender our heart and conscience to the flow of the divine (*divina*) through the reading (*lectio*).

The fundamental principle of *lectio divina* leads us to understand the profound mystery of the Incarnation, "The Word became flesh," not only in history but also within us.

Praying *Lectio* Today

Before you begin, relax your body and maintain a posture of prayer (back straight, eyes shut, feet flat on the floor). Then practice these four simple actions:

1. Read a passage from Scripture or the daily Mass readings. This is known as *lectio*. (If the Word of God is read aloud, the hearers listen attentively.)

2. Pray the selected passage with attention as you listen for a specific meaning that comes to mind. Once again, the reading is listened to or silently read and reflected or meditated on. This is known as *meditatio*.

3. The exercise becomes active. Pick a word, sentence, or idea that surfaces from your consideration of the chosen text. Does the reading remind you of a person, place, or experience? If so, pray about it. Compose your thoughts and reflection into a simple word or phrase. This prayer-thought will help you remove distractions during the *lectio*. This exercise is called *oratio*.

4. In silence, with your eyes closed, quiet yourself and become conscious of your breathing. Let your thoughts, feelings, and concerns fade as you consider the selected passage in the previous step (*oratio*). If you're distracted, use your prayer word to help you return to silence. This is *contemplatio*.

This exercise can take as long as you want, but in the context of this Bible study, 10 to 20 minutes should be sufficient.

Many teachers of prayer call contemplation the prayer of resting in God, a prelude to losing oneself in the presence of God. Scripture is transformed in our hearing as we pray and allow our hearts to unite intimately with the Lord. The Word truly takes on flesh, and this time it is manifested in our flesh.

How to Use This Bible-Study Companion

THE BIBLE, along with the commentaries and reflections found in this study, will help participants become familiar with the Scripture texts and lead them to reflect more deeply on the texts' messages. At the end of this study, participants will have a firm grasp of the Wisdom Books, becoming therefore more aware of the spiritual nourishment these books offer. This study is not only an intellectual adventure, it's also a spiritual one. The reflections lead participants into their own journey with the Scripture readings.

Context

When the authors wrote and edited the Wisdom Books, they were presenting a guide to living wisely and faithfully in God's creation. To help readers learn about each passage in relation to those around it, each lesson begins with an overview that puts the Scripture passages into context.

Part 1: Group Study

To give participants a comprehensive study of the five Wisdom Books, and two other Bible books often associated with them, this study is divided into eight lessons. Lesson 1 is group study only; Lessons 2 through 8 are divided into Part 1, group study, and Part 2, individual study. For example, Lesson 2 covers the Book of Job, chapters 4 through 42. The study group reads and discusses only chapters 4 through 7 (Part 1). Participants privately read and reflect on chapters 8 through 42 (Part 2).

Group study may or may not include *lectio divina*. With *lectio divina,* the group meets for ninety minutes using the first format on page 13. Without *lectio divina,* the group meets for one hour using the format at the bottom of page 13, and participants are urged to privately read the *lectio divina* section at the end of Part 1. It contains additional reflections on the Scripture passages studied during the group session that will take participants even further into the passages.

Part 2: Individual Study

The passages not covered in Part 1 are divided into shorter components, one to be studied each day. Participants who don't belong to a study group can use the lessons for private sacred reading. They may choose to reflect on one Scripture passage per day, making it possible for a clearer understanding of the Scripture passages used in their *lectio divina* (sacred reading).

A PROCESS FOR SACRED READING

Liguori Publications has designed this study to be user-friendly and manageable. However, group dynamics and leaders vary. We're not trying to keep the Holy Spirit from working in your midst, thus we suggest you decide beforehand which format works best for your group. If you have limited time, you could study the Bible as a group and save prayer and reflection for personal time.

However, if your group wishes to digest and feast on sacred Scripture through both prayer and study, we recommend you spend closer to ninety minutes each week by gathering to study and pray with Scripture. *Lectio divina* (see page 8) is an ancient contemplative prayer form that moves readers from the head to the heart in meeting the Lord. We strongly suggest using this prayer form whether in individual or group study.

GROUP-STUDY FORMATS

1. Bible Study With *Lectio Divina*

About ninety minutes of group study

- ✠ Gathering and opening prayer (3–5 minutes)
- ✠ Read each Scripture passage aloud (5 minutes)
- ✠ Silently review the commentary and prepare to discuss it with the group (3–5 minutes)
- ✠ Discuss the Scripture passage along with the commentary and reflection (30 minutes)
- ✠ Read each Scripture passage aloud a second time, followed by quiet time for meditation and contemplation (5 minutes)
- ✠ Spend some time in prayer with the selected passage. Group participants will slowly read the Scripture passage a third time in silence, listening for the voice of God as they read (10–20 minutes)
- ✠ Shared reflection (10–15 minutes)
- ✠ Closing prayer (3–5 minutes)

To become acquainted with lectio divina, *see page 8.*

2. Bible Study

About one hour of group study

- ✠ Gathering and opening prayer (3–5 minutes)
- ✠ Read each Scripture passage aloud (5 minutes)
- ✠ Silently review the commentary and prepare to discuss it with the group (3–5 minutes)
- ✠ Discuss the Scripture passage along with the commentary and reflection (40 minutes)
- ✠ Closing prayer (3–5 minutes)

Notes to the Leader

✠ Bring a copy of the *New American Bible,* revised edition.

✠ Plan which sections will be covered each week of your Bible study.

✠ Read the material in advance of each session.

✠ Establish written ground rules. (Example: We won't keep you longer than ninety minutes; don't dominate the sharing by arguing or debating.)

✠ Meet in an appropriate and welcoming gathering space (church building, meeting room, house).

✠ Provide name tags and perhaps use a brief icebreaker for the first meeting; ask participants to introduce themselves.

✠ Mark the Scripture passage(s) that will be read during the session.

✠ Decide how you would like the Scripture to be read aloud (whether by one or multiple readers).

✠ Use a clock or watch.

✠ Provide extra Bibles (or copies of the Scripture passages) for participants who don't bring their Bible.

✠ Ask participants to read the introduction (page 16) before the first session.

✠ Tell participants which passages to study and urge them to read the passages and commentaries before the meeting.

✠ If you opt to use the *lectio divina* format, familiarize yourself with this prayer form ahead of time.

Notes to the Participants

✠ Bring a copy of the *New American Bible,* revised edition.

✠ Read the introduction (page 16) before the first session.

✠ Read the Scripture passages and commentaries before each session.

✠ Be prepared to share and listen respectfully. (This is not a time to debate beliefs or argue.)

Opening Prayer

Leader: O God, come to my assistance.

Response: O Lord, make haste to help me.

Leader: Glory be to the Father, and to the Son, and to the Holy Spirit...

Response: ...as it was in the beginning, is now, and ever shall be, world without end. Amen.

Leader: Christ is the vine and we are the branches. As branches linked to Jesus, the vine, we are called to recognize that the Scriptures are always being fulfilled in our lives. It is the living Word of God living on in us. Come, Holy Spirit, fill the hearts of your faithful and kindle in us the fire of your divine wisdom, knowledge, and love.

Response: Open our minds and hearts as we study your great love for us as shown in the Bible.

Reader: (Open your Bible to the assigned Scripture(s) and read in a paced, deliberate manner. Pause for one minute, listening for a word, phrase, or image that you may use in your *lectio divina* practice.)

Closing Prayer

Leader: Let us pray as Jesus taught us.

Response: Our Father...

Leader: Lord, inspire us with your Spirit as we study your Word in the Bible. Be with us this day and every day as we strive to know you and serve you and to love as you love. We believe that through your goodness and love, the Spirit of the Lord is truly upon us. Allow the words of the Bible, your Word, to capture us and inspire us to live as you live and to love as you love.

Response: Amen.

Leader: May the divine assistance remain with us always.

Response: In the name of the Father, and of the Son, and of the Holy Spirit. Amen.

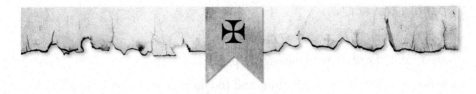

Wisdom Books

JOB, PSALMS, PROVERBS, ECCLESIASTES,
SONG OF SONGS, WISDOM, SIRACH (ECCLESIASTICUS)

Read this overview before the first session.

The Wisdom Books in the Bible are not stories about the patriarchs or the Exodus. Except for several chapters in Ecclesiastes and Sirach, they mention nothing about the Israelites, the monarchy, or the prophets. Many of the writings in the Wisdom Books have their origin in ancient Egyptian, Mesopotamian, and Phoenician writings. Pagan authors, who worshiped idols, penned proverbs about living life in a peaceful and prudent manner. Hebrew writers borrowed from these ancient writings and added a new flavor to them. They wrote about living well and with faith in the one true God who created everything. Thus the Wisdom Books are about instructing readers on how to understand and best deal with the problems of life guided by the spirit of God. Their emphasis is (1) fear of the Lord, and (2) nothing is hidden from the God of Israel who knows everything that is happening in creation.

The Wisdom Books in the Catholic Bible include Job, Proverbs, Ecclesiastes, Wisdom, and Sirach. Although the Book of Psalms and the Song of Songs are not strictly Wisdom Books, their strong association with the other five books allow them to be included as such in the Catholic Bible and hence in this volume as well.

The Book of Job speaks of suffering and the need to trust God in the midst of our suffering. It attempts to explain why bad things happen to good people.

The Book of Psalms contains the prayers of saintly Old Testament writers who used songs to express their love of God. The Book of Psalms includes a collection of liturgical songs, poetry, lamentations, thanksgiving prayers, and petitions for the Lord to curse the enemies of the Israelites.

The Book of Proverbs communicates practical wisdom for living a life faithful to the Lord and in accord with prudent human relationships.

The Book of Ecclesiastes (Qoheleth), a cynical book, stresses the vanities of life and the reality that nothing is new under the sun.

The Song of Songs uses erotic images to illustrate God's intimate relationship with the Chosen People.

The Book of Wisdom personifies Wisdom as an attractive woman worthy of praise. It speaks of the rewards received by the righteous, and the punishment of the wicked, especially those who worship false idols.

The Book of Sirach (Ecclesiasticus) has wise sayings, hymns to wisdom, sensible counsel, and reflections on the human condition.

Fear of the Lord

Fear of the Lord is an expression found often in the Scriptures, especially in the Wisdom Books, which tell us fear of the Lord is the beginning of wisdom. Fear of the Lord in this context does not mean a terrorizing fear of a judgmental God It refers to the reverence and awe a person has for God who is a wise, just, merciful, and loving God, who sees all. Reverence and awe before God is the beginning of wisdom and the foundation for our desire to know, love, and serve God and to live a life faithful to the Lord.

NOTE: Due to the vast amount of material in the Wisdom Books, this commentary will present a major sampling of the proverbs and counsels found in the books without commenting on all the material in the books. The sampling is intended to offer those studying the text a solid familiarity with the writings in the Wisdom Books.

The Book of Job (I)

JOB 1–3

Naked I came forth from my mother's womb, and naked shall I go back there. The LORD gave and the LORD has taken away; blessed be the name of the LORD! (1:21).

Opening Prayer (SEE PAGE 15)

Context

Job 1—3 The Book of Job, composed between the seventh and fifth centuries before Christ, is named after a man named Job, the central character of the book. The book pictures the suffering of Job as a test to prove his love and goodness before God, but it does not totally answer the question why bad things happen to good people. The name Job means, "Where is the divine father?" It is a fitting name for the events that take place in the book. Knowing he has remained faithful to the Lord throughout his life, Job will struggle with the question of why he is being punished. Despite the advice of his friends telling him he must have sinned, he defends his innocence. He longs to speak with the Lord face to face so he can defend himself.

Job is an innocent, rich, and God-fearing man. God is pleased with Job because of his faithfulness and, believing Job will remain faithful even in adversity, God gives permission to the adversary (the satan) to test Job by taking away his children and his possessions and causing Job to be covered with boils. Three friends of Job come to comfort him and are shocked at his gaunt appearance and his profound discouragement. Job experiences deep depression about his situation.

PART 1: GROUP STUDY (JOB 1—3)

Read aloud Job 1—3.

1—2 Job's Plight

The story begins in the Land of Uz, east of Palestine, in Arabia, where Job—a pious, God-fearing man—is living an idealistic life, blessed by the Lord with seven sons and three daughters, 7,000 sheep, 3,000 camels, 500 yoke of oxen, 500 she-donkeys, and a very large household, making him superior to anyone in the East. Because Job lived in the land of Uz, he is not portrayed as an Israelite. Job's sons would take turns hosting feasts to which they invited their sisters and ate and drank with them.

Although others apparently joined in the parties, Job's major concern is for his children. After each party, fearing they offended the Lord, Job would sanctify them, offering sacrifices to the Lord on their behalf.

The story turns abruptly to the heavenly court of the Lord, referred to as the "sons of God." In ancient times, many of the people viewed the Lord as seeking counsel from a heavenly group (angels) who were referred to as the sons of God and who could sin and challenge the Lord. During the gathering, "the satan" also comes among them after patrolling the earth. Although many readers will immediately identify the satan with the devil, the name actually means "adversary," and only later in the Bible will the title be applied to the devil who is presented as an opponent of the Lord, not one of the heavenly court. "The satan" is not a name but a description given to the one testing Job. The Bible speaks of the satan without a capital letter in its title to stress it simply refers to one's role, not one's name.

In the story of Job, the satan acts more like a prosecuting attorney, intent on testing the faithfulness of Job. In the heavenly court, the Lord boasts about the faithfulness of Job. The adversary declares Job is faithful because the Lord has blessed him with such abundance. He challenges the Lord to take away all Job's possesses, predicting Job will curse the Lord when this occurs. In response, the Lord turns Job over to the satan, allowing the adversary to do whatever he wishes to do to Job with the exception of laying a hand on Job.

Job's idealistic life suddenly changes when he receives news from a survivor that the Sabeans captured all Job's oxen and donkeys and killed all his servants. A second survivor arrives and reports about fire from heaven, possibly a reference to lightning, striking and killing Job's sheep and the servants. A third survivor then arrives, reporting the Chaldeans carried off all Job's camels and killed all the servants. Finally, a fourth survivor arrives and reports the most shattering news of all. A strong wind came across the desert and destroyed the house in which Job's sons and daughters were eating and drinking, killing all the young people in the house. Job's wife is not mentioned yet. She will appear later.

Job mourns the loss of all his possessions and family, but he continues to worship the Lord, declaring he came naked from his mother's womb and knows he will return to the earth naked, meaning he will die with no possessions. In the midst of total loss, Job neither sinned nor accused God of doing wrong.

Chapter 2 begins with another meeting of the heavenly court, "the sons of God." The Lord continues to praise the unsurpassed faithfulness of Job, who remains faithful despite the ruin the Lord inflicted on him at the urging of the adversary. Although the Lord gave the satan the right to do to Job whatever he wished, the text reveals the Lord is the only one who has the power to inflict whatever the satan wants. Blessings and curses are still within the Lord's power, not in the power of the satan. Rather than blame the Lord for the affliction endured by Job, the story places the responsibility on the satan.

The satan applies an expression usually used in bartering: "skin for skin!" Its use here is not clear, but the adversary seems to be saying a man will give all he has for his life, meaning nothing is more important to a person than health and one's life. The satan challenges the Lord to afflict the bones and flesh of Job, believing Job will then curse the Lord. As before, the Lord declares Job is in the hands of the adversary, but he must spare Job's life.

The adversary then afflicts Job with severe boils "from the soles of his feet to the crown of his head" (2:7). Job sits among ashes, a sign of mourning for the affliction he is enduring. Job's wife scoffs at his foolish innocence, tempting him to curse God and die. The implication is one who curses God would immediately be struck dead. Job's wife is saying he has nothing more to live for. Job rebukes her, calling her a foolish woman. The term "foolish" could mean she was an unbelieving woman. He defends his faith in the Lord, saying, "We accept good things from God; should we not accept evil?" (2:10).

When three of Job's friends heard about the misfortune he endured, they set out to console him. Eliphaz came from Teman, which is in Edom. The people of Teman were noted for their wisdom. Bildad came from Shuh, and Zophar came from Naamath. The locations of these last two places are unknown. When Job's three friends met him and did not recognize him in his grief, they immediately began their ritual of mourning, weeping aloud, tearing their cloaks, throwing dust into the air over their heads, and sitting with Job in silence on the ground for the usual period of mourning of seven days and seven nights.

3 Job's Complaint

Job never curses the Lord, but curses "his day," a reference to the day of his birth. He wishes the day he was born would disappear, a day when the good news of the birth of a boy would never have happened, a day to be lost in darkness, with the Lord forgetting about it, and a day fading into darkness and gloom, erased from the numbering of the days or months. He wished the night of his birth to be empty, with no cry of joy sounding in it.

Imploring those who curse the sea, those who have the ability to rouse up Leviathan, a mythological sea monster, Job asks them to join him in cursing the day of his birth. He asks why he did not die at birth, why he was well-born and nursed. He views death as a tranquil experience, a place where he would rest with kings and princes. His image of death did not include punishment or reward, but a state where the wicked cease from evil, the weary rest, captives live at ease, and the servant is freed from the master. It is the end of everything.

Review Questions

1. Who is "the satan" in the story of Job? Is the satan presented as an evil person?
2. What does the author mean when he refers to a heavenly court with the Lord?
3. What wisdom lesson does Job teach when he loses everything?

Closing Prayer (SEE PAGE 15)

Pray the closing prayer now or after *lectio divina*.

Lectio Divina (SEE PAGE 8)

Relax your body and maintain a posture of prayer (back straight, eyes shut, feet flat on the floor). This exercise can take as long as you want, but in the context of this Bible study, 10 to 20 minutes should be sufficient.

The meditations that follow are provided only to help group participants use this prayer form, but note that *lectio* is intended to bring one to a place of prayerful contemplation where the Word of God speaks to the hearer from his or her heart. (See page 8 for further instruction.)

Job's Plight (1—2)

Job realizes God has blessed us in many ways, and we gratefully accept these good gifts, but we must also accept the fact that life is not always easy. Job says, "We accept good things from God; should we not accept evil?" (2:10).

✠ *What can I learn from this passage?*

Job's Complaint (3)

Job reflects the reaction of many people of faith to a major disaster in their life. They may wish for death, feeling the emotional loss is too much for them to bear. Like Job, people thrown into the depths of despondency do not abandon God but become more aware of the need for faith in their life.

✠ *What can I learn from this passage?*

The Book of Job (II)

JOB 4–42

By hearsay I had heard of you, but now my eye has seen you. Therefore I disown what I have said, and repent in dust and ashes (42:5–6).

Opening Prayer (SEE PAGE 15)

Context

Part 1: Job 4—7 Each of Job's friends speaks to him in a series of speeches, attempting to convince Job of his sinfulness and to encourage him to repent so the Lord will bless him. In these chapters, Eliphaz, one of Job's friends, refuses to blame God for Job's condition. In his reply, Job refuses to admit he has done anything sinful.

Part 2: Job 8—42 Job's three friends deliver three speeches to him, saying he must have sinned. Job replies to each, denying any guilt. A young man attempts to address Job, and he receives the same results as Job's three friends. The Lord finally challenges Job, who accepts the Lord's rebuke. The Lord eventually rewards Job for remaining faithful in the midst of his suffering.

PART 1: GROUP STUDY (JOB 4—7)

Read aloud Job 4—7.

4—5 Eliphaz's First Speech

Each of the speeches usually begins with a question and a reference to Job's remarks. The first of Job's friends, Eliphaz, begins the first cycle of speeches by asking Job if he would mind if someone attempts to speak with him. He begins gently, reminding Job how his (Job's) instruction helped and strengthened many people. Now, however, when Job finds himself experiencing grief, he becomes impatient and disillusioned. Bidding Job to seek strength in his piety and integrity, Eliphaz urges him to recall that the Lord does not punish innocent people.

In a confusing passage that seems out of place and may have resulted from a later addition, Eliphaz speaks of a terrifying vision of a figure who asks if anyone can be more in the right than God. The unspoken answer is "no." Since the Lord's servants and messengers in the heavenly court cannot be blameless, how can those on earth be blameless?

In chapter 5, Eliphaz warns Job not to be impatient or resentful like a fool who imparts his foolishness to his household and children. He declares that trust in human beings alone is foolish and urges Job to state his case before God, the Lord over the earth and all human beings.

Eliphaz attempts to soothe Job, noting those whom the Lord reproves are blessed. He believes God does not discipline a person as a sign of rejection but for healing and repentance. The Lord may be punishing Job to eventually protect him from famine, war, or malicious speech. If Job can accept this, he will scoff at all adversity, knowing his household is secure. Eliphaz insists this is what he learned throughout his many years and what Job himself should know.

6—7 Job's First Reply

Job responds by speaking of the depth of his anguish, which has become heavier than the sand of the sea. Instead of seeking an abundance of blessings from the Lord, Job, at this point, seeks only to die and be free from anguish. His only consolation is his belief he has not sinned against the Lord.

Job rejects Eliphaz's comments, accusing him of speaking words that offer no help. Like caravans seeking refreshment in the desert, Job discovers no refreshing water in Eliphaz's words and finds himself perishing. He seeks nothing from his friends except knowledge about what he did wrong. If they can tell him, he will remain silent. He begs them to stop ignoring his statements about his innocence.

In chapter 7, Job speaks of the drudgery of life, comparing it to the life of a hireling or a slave. In his misery, he suffers sleepless nights and complains about his sores and the swift passing of hopeless days, informing his friends he will soon be gone down to Sheol, the place of the dead.

Job turns his attention to God, asking if he (Job) is a monster needing to be watched. When he seeks the comfort of sleep, the Lord frightens him with dreams and visions to the point he would rather be strangled to death than continue to exist. Since he expects to die soon, he begs the Lord to pardon him and remove his guilt so he may die in peace.

Review Questions

1. What advice does Eliphaz give to Job?
2. Why did Job feel Eliphaz was no help to him?
3. What are some sufferings endured by Job?

Closing Prayer (SEE PAGE 15)

Pray the closing prayer now or after *lectio divina*.

Lectio Divina (SEE PAGE 8)

Relax your body and maintain a posture of prayer (back straight, eyes shut, feet flat on the floor). This exercise can take as long as you want, but in the context of this Bible study, 10 to 20 minutes should be sufficient.

The meditations that follow are provided only to help group participants use this prayer form, but note that *lectio* is intended to bring one to a place of prayerful contemplation where the Word of God speaks to the hearer from his or her heart. (See page 8 for further instruction.)

Eliphaz's First Speech (4—5)

Jesus had to correct some false beliefs of the people of ancient Israel, among them the idea that punishment is a sign of God's disfavor. Following the common thinking of his day, Eliphaz believes Job's punishment comes as a result of Job's sinfulness. Jesus, however, said the Lord "makes his sun rise on the bad and the good, and causes rain to fall on the just and the unjust" (Matthew 5:45). According to Jesus, good and evil people experience the same joys and difficulties in creation. Spiritual writers say it is not what happens to us that matters, but how we respond to what happens to us.

✠ *What can I learn from this passage?*

Job's First Reply (6—7)

Job became deeply despondent over the loss of his family and possessions, but he remained faithful to the Lord. Many of the saints went through periods of suffering, doubt, great loss, and temptations to despair and they became saints because they remained faithful to God during such periods, as Job did. Depression, doubt, and despondency are not sins, but part of the struggle toward sainthood.

✠ *What can I learn from this passage?*

PART 2: INDIVIDUAL STUDY (JOB 8—42)

Day 1: The First Cycle of Speeches (8—14)

Bildad, the second companion, asks Job how long will he speak about such things. He declares the words Job speaks are like a mighty wind. If Job's children sinned, Job can still pray and the Lord will listen to his plea if he is blameless.

Bildad declares they all have the wisdom of their ancestors. The lessons of the past teach about the lack of hope in those who abandon the Lord. Those who reject the Lord may seem strong and healthy during life, but when they die, they are forgotten. God, however, will reward the upright and fill their lives with joy. Those who hate the Lord will find shame and destruction.

In chapter 9, Job agrees with Bildad concerning God's protection of the good, and he asks who could contend with God and answer even one question out of a thousand God may ask. He stresses God's power over the mountains, the earth and its foundations, the sun, the stars, the heavens, the sea, and the constellations. He declares the Lord is unseen and performs many miracles. Although the Lord also brings death, no one dares to ask the Lord to explain what is happening. Job does not believe he could argue his case with the Lord even if he were right.

Feeling helpless before the Lord, Job speaks as though the Lord decided to punish him, whether he is good or evil. If he decided to forget his complaints against God and acted cheerfully, the Lord would still overwhelm him with even more sorrows, since he would not be telling the truth. Since the Lord will not accept his claim of innocence, he asks in frustration why he should try to speak with the Lord.

Since the Lord is not human as he is, Job feels he has no way to discuss the problem fairly with the Lord. He wishes an arbiter would be able to act between them so the arbiter could free him from the punishing rod of the Lord. If the Lord would at least cease punishing him, he would be able to speak to the Lord without fear and boldly defend his innocence. Since this is not happening, Job declares he hates his life.

In chapter 10, Job continues his rant against God, complaining about the bitterness he feels and his helplessness before the power of the Lord. He continues to beg God to tell him why he is being oppressed, sarcastically asking if the Lord enjoys oppressing him. He asks whether the Lord is unjust like human beings, searching for sins he did not commit, just to prove people cannot save themselves from the hand of the Lord.

In an effort to understand, he asks whether the Lord created him to destroy him if he sinned, not counting Job's good deeds. He admits the Lord gave him life and love, but these are now hidden in the heart of the Lord. In frustration, he asks why the Lord intended this misery, allowing him to be born rather than causing his death at the time of birth. He begs the Lord to leave him alone so he may enjoy a small moment of comfort before he enters the land of darkness in death.

In chapter 11, Zophar, the third speaker, questions if Job's tirade against the Lord should be left unchallenged. He mocks Job, whom, he says, appears to think he is pure in the eyes of the Lord yet who is actually ignoring some of his own wickedness. He asks if Job thinks he is able to judge God, as though Job knows the mind and motives of the Almighty, who is without guilt. Zophar urges Job to remove all wickedness from himself so he can face God innocently and in peace. If Job repents, his misery will cease and he will live with security and hope, able to aid others who seek his help.

In chapter 12, Job replies for a third time, acknowledging the wisdom of his friends, but adding he too has wisdom. Claiming he is being mocked by his neighbors who say the just and perfect Job is disgraced, he points to robbers and the wicked as examples of people who receive security from the Lord. The dumbest creatures of the earth know the Lord is in control of creation. Job says just as wisdom and understanding accompany old age, so the Lord has wisdom, might, and understanding, yet whatever the Lord decides to do in all creation must take place.

In chapter 13, Job rants against his three friends, calling them worthless physicians who would be wise to remain silent. Since they are attempting to defend the Lord with their false accusations, he calls their advice "ashy maxims." He tells them to remain silent and let him speak to the Lord, defending himself even if the Lord would slay him. Again, he asks what his sins are, pleading with the Lord not to turn away from him or to shackle him.

In chapter 14, Job speaks of the life span of human beings as being short. Since his life is so short, he asks the Lord not to bring him to judgment but to let him live his life. He points to a tree when it is cut down. The tree's stump will sprout again when watered, even if it dies in the dust. When a man dies, his life ends, never to be taken up again. Job asks to be hidden alive in Sheol (the land of the dead) until the Lord's wrath against him ends. Then the Lord could lift him up and not treat him like a sinner. When people die, they learn nothing more about their children, whether they are honored or disgraced.

Lectio Divina

Spend 8 to 10 minutes in silent contemplation of the following passage:

> For Job, losing all his possessions was painful, but losing the feeling God loved him added to his pain. The saints often endure a spiritual

experience known as "the dark night of the soul." Like Job, they feel abandoned by God and have great difficulty praying. During this period, God appears to be absent and seems to ignore them. Saints, however, keep praying, no matter how far away God seems to be.

✠ *What can I learn from this passage?*

Day 2: The Second Cycle of Speeches (15—21)

Eliphaz begins the second cycle of speeches, asking if a wise man would respond like Job with windy, puffed up, and useless wisdom. He accuses Job of abandoning piety and devotion before God, saying his own words condemn him. Questioning the source of Job's wisdom, Eliphaz asks Job if he were born before the hills were created, or whether he belonged to the heavenly council before the creation of the world, or whether he knows more than those more advanced in age than his father. He rebukes Job for becoming angry against God, who does not trust the wisdom of the holy ones in the heavenly council, much less the wisdom of human beings. Eliphaz calls attention to the wisdom of the ancients who teach that the wicked, because they challenged the Almighty, will live a short life in torment.

In chapter 16, Job accuses his friends of offering only disturbing comfort with words that rattle on, admitting he would be saying the same thing if he were in their place. He claims the Lord has worn him down, shriveled him up, torn him apart in anger, and left him a prey to the wicked. Using material images to express his feelings of abandonment, he claims the Lord broke him in two, snatched him by the neck, smashed him to pieces, and made him a target for arrows. He bids the earth not to cover his blood so his innocent blood can incessantly call out to God. The people of ancient times believed the blood of the innocent calls out to the Lord, even after death. In the Book of Genesis, the Lord accuses Cain of killing Abel, saying, "Your brother's blood cries out to me from the ground!" (Genesis 4:10).

Despite Job's bitter words against the Lord, Job begs God to bring him justice. He accepts his place in life, speaking as a mere mortal who will live only so long before he travels to his death, from which there is no return. The people of Job's day did not believe in life after death.

In chapter 17, Job declares he is surrounded by people who mock him and spit on him. He is just a shadow of his former self, shocking the innocent who see him. Since he finds no wisdom in his companions who refuse to believe his innocence, he urges them to leave. His only hope is the darkness of the grave and its decay.

In chapter 18, Bildad questions Job as to when his babbling will end. He urges Job to reflect on his situation and accuses Job of treating his friends like animals. He states the wicked live in darkness, deceived by their own ideas, falling into snares, surrounded by terror, hungry for strength, skin decaying, on the doorstep of death. They have no offspring to keep their memory alive. Although Bildad does not name Job as being among the wicked when speaking about the suffering in store for evil people, he is implying Job belongs among the wicked.

In chapter 19, Job objects to Bildad's implied accusation, saying he would know if he were a sinner. Job continues to accuse the Lord of dealing unfairly with him, toying with him as though he were caught in a net. Using military images, he accuses the Lord of counting him as an enemy, advancing troops against him, encamping misery around his life. His family and closest friends loath and avoid him. He hopes to be proven innocent, even if he has already died and his skin totally decayed. Being remembered after death as an honorable person was important to the people of Job's era. Job warns those accusing him of guilt their anger could be their sin.

In chapter 20, Zophar the Naamathite begins his second speech by asking in verse 5 if Job does not know that "the triumph of the wicked is short," despite their arrogant pride. Like his friends, Zophar stresses the afflictions accompanying evil and declares the end of the wicked is like dung used for fuel. Their prosperity will not save their life. Their children will live among the poor, experiencing in their own household the gloomy punishment for wickedness.

In chapter 21, Job argues with Zophar's idea about the afflictions of the wicked. For Job, reality provides a different picture. Good people suffer and die, and the wicked continue to live. The progeny of the wicked flourishes in their offspring, their homes are safe, they are not punished by God, their animals breed successfully, they live in joy with their families, and they die in peace. They have no desire to know God, asking who the Almighty is that they should serve such a God. Job questions whether God is storing up a person's misery for the person's children. If so, it means nothing when the wicked person is in the grave.

Job admits no one can question God's wisdom. One dies in good health and another dies without any happiness in life. Both lie in the dust together. During times of disaster, the evil man is spared, and when he dies, he is gloriously carried to the place of burial where someone keeps watch over his grave. Job asks, in light of such reality, how Zophar's words could comfort him.

Lectio Divina

Spend 8 to 10 minutes in silent contemplation of the following passage:

When Job needed people to understand him, his closest friends misunderstood him completely, adding to his misery. Jesus experienced a similar misery when Judas, a close companion, betrayed him. Not only did the physical suffering harm Jesus, but the emotional betrayal of a friend he loved intensified his passion. When someone is suffering, a faithful friend is a great comfort and blessing, and an unfaithful friend is another thorn in one's side.

✠ *What can I learn from this passage?*

Day 3: The Third Cycle of Speeches (22—28)

Eliphaz begins his third speech asking if the Lord—who needs nothing— profits anything from human beings. Believing only the wicked receive punishment, Eliphaz sarcastically asks Job if it is his justice or piety provoking the Lord to reprove him. Ironically, it is Job's piety and justice that prompted his adversary, the satan, to test him.

Listing sins inadvertently committed by the rich, Eliphaz accuses Job of gaining his wealth sinfully by not sharing with the hungry or thirsty, ignoring the needs of widows and orphans, and acting as though the land belongs only to the powerful. Eliphaz asks if Job believes God cannot see his sins. Challenging Job's assertion that sinners prosper, Eliphaz points to sins of the past where the wicked were swept away by a flood and the just rejoiced.

He pleads with Job to intercede with the Lord who will hear his plea.

In chapter 23, Job responds, wishing he could present his case in person before the Lord and learn firsthand the intent of the Lord's punishment. He believes the Lord listens to the arguments of the just and blesses them and laments he cannot find the Lord in all the earth. Although he can claim he remained faithful to the Lord's command and has been tested like gold, he knows no one can contend with the decisions of the Lord, which, he admits, terrify him.

In chapter 24, Job again questions why the Lord's friends do not witness the punishment deserved by the wicked. He lists the sins the wicked inflict on the poor, the widow, and the orphan. They steal the possessions of the poor, their land, their herds, their donkeys, their oxen, and take their infants as collateral for a debt. Despite the plight of the oppressed, the Lord appears to do nothing against the wicked. Verses 18 to 24 in this chapter are unclear and may be a later insertion.

In chapter 25, Bildad delivers a short speech concerning the power of the Lord, asking how anyone can fight against the numerous troops of the Lord. How can anyone be innocent and right before the Lord? Compared to the glory of the Lord, the moon and the stars lack brilliance.

In chapter 26, Job asks Bildad how one can give counsel to those without wisdom. He stresses the power of the Lord by presenting a cosmic view of the world, using the common images of the universe at the time the author of Job penned this book. The shades (the dead in the Sheol) writhe in terror. The Lord covers the earth with the firmament and suspends the earth over nothing, while the clouds carry the weight of the waters without being split open like overloaded balloons. The Lord blankets the moon with clouds and sets the boundaries for the seas and for the days and nights.

The foundations of the earth tremble at the thunderous rebuke of the Lord, who then calms the sea and crushes Rahab (a primeval sea monster) and the fleeing serpent, both symbols of chaos. Through the movement of the wind, the Lord clears up the heavens. Since these are just a whisper of the power of the Lord, Job asks who would dare attempt to understand the thunder of the Lord's power.

In chapter 27, Job claims he will never deny his innocence, even though

God has made his life bitter. He finds no reason to reproach himself for his stance. Because the wicked plead with the Lord only in times of crisis, the Lord will not listen to their prayer. Despite the number of children the wicked have, they will be buried in death with no one to weep for them. The rich man's house and wealth shall be like a heap of dust. Although the wicked may attempt to flee from the power of the grave, they will still die.

Chapter 28 is a poem about the futility of the attempt of human beings to discover true wisdom. Human beings are capable of breaking open shafts and mine into the dark earth to find silver, iron, gold, and fine jewels. They know how to dam up streams in search of gold, but they do not know how to discover wisdom. She is not in the depths of the sea, nor can gold, silver, or precious stones purchase her. Wisdom is known only by God, who sees the ends of the earth, sends the wind, makes boundaries for the waters, and brings the rain and thunderbolts. The Lord established wisdom, scrutinized her, and proclaimed "the fear of the Lord is wisdom" (v. 28) and the avoidance of evil, understanding.

Lectio Divina

Spend 8 to 10 minutes in silent contemplation of the following passage:

There is a story about the gods wishing to hide true wisdom from human beings. They thought of hiding it in the highest heaven, in the deepest sea, in the wind, and even in hell, but as they named each place, they realized human beings would search everything and would find it. In desperation, one of the gods suggested they hide the truth (wisdom) deep within people. Even if they find it, they will not believe it. The gods laughed and agreed with this idea. In the Book of Job, we learn true wisdom is known only by God who shares it with human beings.

✠ *What can I learn from this passage?*

Day 4: Job's Final Summary of His Cause (Job 29—31)

Job recalls the days when God walked with him like a lamp lighting his way through the darkness. He prospered under the shelter of the Almighty, with his children all around him and his oil flowed in abundance. At the city gate, the young stepped aside for him and the elders stood up when he approached. Princes and the highest officials stood in silence in his presence. He helped the poor, the orphans, the dying, widows, the blind, and the lame. Strangers received a fair trial, and the wicked were forced to free their victims. Job expected to live a long life and die quietly. He corrected the people like their leader, living like a king in the midst of his army and like one who comforts mourners.

In chapter 30, Job laments over the children of the wicked. Although they have strong backs, they are driven from the community and huddle in the wastelands, in ravines and caves, eating roots and leaves. Now he is like them. Job finds himself the subject of the vulgar songs of the wicked, despised, and spit upon. He becomes deeply depressed, racked with pain, rapidly losing weight, and cast off by the Lord. He accuses God of being his tormentor, leading him to his death. Recalling the help he gave to the poor, he expected blessing for his deeds, but instead he received evil, with his skin black and peeling, his bones burning with fever, and a heavy heart.

In chapter 31, Job challenges the Lord to weigh him on a scale of justice, believing he would be found innocent. If any stain of sin is found in him, he declares his crops deserve to be eaten by another. If he allows his eyes and heart to roam and commits a sin with his neighbor's wife, he deserves punishment, accepting the verdict his wife should become the wife of another. For any sins he could have committed, he deserves to be sent into the valley of destruction.

Job continues to list one sin after the other. If he refused justice to his servants when they had a just complaint against him, or denied the poor what they needed, or allowed a widow to languish while he ate his portion alone, or ignored the orphan, or withheld a covering from a poor person, or raised his hand against the innocent, or put his trust in gold, or worshiped the sun and the moon, thus denying God, or rejoiced at the destruction of an enemy, or invoked a curse against his enemies' life, or hidden his sins, then he would justly receive punishment from the Lord. He wants to read what the accuser is saying against him, and if proven true, he will wear it for all to see. Wishing he had someone to hear his case, he called upon the Almighty to answer him.

Like a prince, Job is willing to present himself before the Lord. If his land cries out against him, if he has eaten its strength without repayment, if he has grieved the hearts of its tenant farmers, then let thorns grow instead of wheat and stinkweed instead of barley.

The passage ends with the statement: "The words of Job are ended."

Lectio Divina

Spend 8 to 10 minutes in silent contemplation of the following passage:

Job could recall the days he felt the Lord walked with him, lighting up his way. There are times in prayer when the Lord touches our heart and allows us to experience a deep love and dedication to God. God is so close. There are other times when we experience a dry period in prayer, a time when we must struggle to keep our thoughts on God. The memory of the former blessings in prayer can carry us through dry periods. Recalling his past experiences of the Lord's presence helped Job through his desolation.

✠ *What can I learn from this passage?*

Day 5: Elihu's Speeches (32—37)

When Job's three companions realized Job would not change his stance about his innocence, they no longer conversed with him. A young man named Elihu, who remained silent because he was younger than the three, became angry with Job for considering himself to be innocent before God and with the three companions for not finding a good answer with which to condemn Job. He asserts wisdom comes, not with old age, but from God and declares he listened intently to the three men and noted none of them could refute Job.

The young man boasts he would not have answered Job in the weak way Job's three friends did. Elihu likens himself to an unopened wine, like wineskin near bursting. He hopes to find relief by replying to Job, protesting he shows no partiality or flattery to anyone. The Lord would strike him dead if he spoke in that manner.

In chapter 33, Elihu approaches Job as a friend, a human being whom Job need not fear. Recalling Job's obstinate protests of innocence and his complaint the Lord never answers him, he views his role as a type of mediator between Job and God. He tells Job the Lord speaks to people in dreams and night visions, inspiring them with wisdom and instruction, keeping them from becoming proud, and warning them about the penalties of sin.

If God wishes, God may chastise people with pain or sickness so they lose their appetite, become skin and bone, and live close to death. At such a time, God may send a messenger to rejuvenate them. Elihu, like Job's three friends, tells Job the Lord answers the prayer of people who repent and returns them to their former life. If Job has nothing to say, he is to keep silent and let Elihu teach him wisdom.

In chapter 34, Elihu speaks to Job's friends, addressing them as wise out of respect for their age. He says that just as the ear and the palate choose what is good, so they should all choose what is right and good. Because Job proclaims his innocence, Elihu accuses him of blasphemy and being a companion of evildoers. He challenges Job's belief that there is no profit in pleasing God, claiming God, the Almighty, can do no wrong. God, who rules over the world and keeps it in existence, cannot act with wickedness.

Elihu notes, if God so wished, God could make humans turn to dust in a second. He states Job, whom he views as an enemy of justice, cannot be in control. Human beings, no matter how powerful, are destined to die. Even in the densest darkness, evil people cannot hide from God. If God is silent or hides from view, no one can complain. Elihu accuses Job of lacking knowledge and deserving punishment because he sins even more in rejecting his (Elihu's) sound arguments and denying his sinfulness.

In chapter 35, Elihu castigates Job for declaring he, not God, is right and for asking what his innocence has profited him. Inviting Job to behold the vast heavens created by the Lord, he asks Job what his offenses or good actions do to God. In anguish, the oppressed call out to God, who makes human beings wiser than beasts and birds, and they often receive no answer. It is foolish to say God does not hear or act. God will help those who wait patiently. Elihu declares Job to be acting without true knowledge of God when he complains about the way God is punishing him.

In chapter 36, Elihu continues to instruct Job about God, declaring he (Elihu) has perfect knowledge of his subject. He tells Job that God is great and just in judging the wicked and providing for the poor. God raises the just to places of honor, on thrones with kings, while the wrath of God punishes the wicked and arrogant, making them aware of their sins. If they listen to God and repent, they will prosper, but if they do not listen, they will perish in their ignorance. God entices the wicked to repent and share in a glorious life, but those who refuse to abandon their anger, like Job, choose evil.

Continuing to respond to Job's tirade against God, Elihu speaks of the power and goodness of God. Who could teach as the Lord does or who would dare accuse God of doing wrong? Elihu tells Job to praise God, whose greatness surpasses human knowledge and collects the water droplets for rain. Through God's magnificent power over nature, God punishes the people or blesses them with abundance. The lightning shaft is in the hands of God and strikes its target as God wills.

In chapter 37, Elihu speaks of the enormous power of God over nature. Thunder, lightning, rain, and sun are subject to the power of God. God's voice roars like thunder over the earth, and bolts of lightning flash across the entire earth. God commands the snow and rain to fall. Elihu mocks Job, asking him to instruct them if he is so wise. He compares God's glory to the sun, which can be seen when the winds sweep the clouds away, yet which can blind one's eye. Elihu ends his argument, saying people fear God whom no one can see, no matter how much wisdom a person may possess.

Lectio Divina

Spend 8 to 10 minutes in silent contemplation of the following passage:

Job can agree with Elihu's image of a marvelous God, but because he knows a loving and compassionate God, he is confused. Why is God punishing him? The Book of Job answers the question of suffering in general. Love for God is not tested by prosperity but by one's faithfulness to a loving God, in good times and in bad.

✠ *What can I learn from this passage?*

Day 6: The Lord and Job Meet (38—42)

God speaks to Job from the whirlwind, a typical setting used when the Lord speaks to humans. God is harsh with Job. The Lord asks where Job was when the foundation of the earth was established. Mocking Job, God asks him who determined the size of the earth, created the stars, set boundaries for the waters on the earth, established limits for night and morning, shattered the pride of the wicked, knew the sources of the sea, understood about death, and measured the size of the earth. If Job is wise enough to know the answer to these questions, then God cynically asks him to share this knowledge.

The Lord continues to challenge Job, asking where light and darkness dwell, where snow and hail reside, where the winds split apart, who determined the direction of the rain and thunderstorms, who gave birth to ice and frost, and who created the stars. God challenges the power of Job, asking if he has power over the laws of the earth, commanding the clouds and the lightning.

In chapter 39, God continues to test Job's knowledge, using the habits of animals to question Job. Does Job know when mountain goats are born or the number of months a deer must wait before she gives birth? Has Job given freedom from family bonds to the donkey and other animals? Would Job trust the powerful ox to bring in the harvest alone? God recognizes the need for humans to practice some control in creation. Because an ostrich lacks wisdom, she uncaringly abandons her eggs in the sand where someone may step on them. God asks Job if Job gave the warhorse its strength or its courage and prowess in battle, and if Job commanded the eagle to build its nest up high where he can watch for food for his young.

In chapter 40, God asks if Job still wishes to argue with the Almighty. A subdued Job replies he accounts for little and puts his hand over his mouth. He declares he has already said too much.

The Lord chides Job, asking if he is able to condemn the Lord to show himself justified and if he is as strong as God, able to roar with a voice like thunder. If so, then God sarcastically invites him to clothe himself in grandeur and majesty, venting his fury, disgracing the proud with a glance, overpowering the wicked, and burying them in the dust. These powers belong to God, but if Job can do them, then the Lord will praise him for recognizing his (Job's) own strength will save him.

The Lord invites Job to look at Behemoth, whom God has created, a primeval monster of chaos that some scholars identify as a hippopotamus or a crocodile. He eats grass, possesses powerful muscles, with a tail as straight as a cedar, a back like bronze tubes, and limbs like iron rods. Only God dare approach him without a sword. He eats the plants of the wild and preys on animals. He hides in the weeds near streams, undisturbed when the rivers grow violent, even when the swelling Jordan surges up to his mouth.

The Lord asks who could control such an animal as Leviathan, another monster of chaos, or put a ring through its nose to lead it around. Will the monster agree to a covenant, accept the role of a slave, speak with soft words, transform into a pet to play with little girls, be traded among merchants, or be captured with barbs or spears for catching fish? Those who fight with him will recognize no other conflict to be as difficult as this.

In chapter 41, the Lord continues to speak. Since no one except God dares to stand before Leviathan, who would dare to stand before the Lord? Everything under the heavens belongs to God. Only the Lord can penetrate the monster's tough outer skin. Rows of scales cover the monster's back, and when he sneezes, light flashes from him. Smoke comes from his nostrils and his hot breath can ignite fires. He is powerful, causing terror wherever he goes, even to the gods. No weapon can stop him. The waters churn up after him like a path of white hair, and there is no one on earth like him. He is the king of all proud beasts.

In chapter 42, Job expresses his belief that the Lord can do all things, and no one can hinder the plans of the Lord. Job admits he spoke without truly understanding some things too marvelous for him to understand. He heard of the Lord in the past, but now he has seen God and repents of all he said.

In an epilogue to the Book of Job, the Lord expresses anger with Job's three friends, telling them to take seven bulls and seven rams to Job and to sacrifice them as a burnt offering for themselves and to let Job pray for his friends. A burnt offering was one fully consumed as an offering to the Lord. The men did as the Lord commanded and showed favor to Job. Elihu is not mentioned as having to make an offering.

After Job prayed for his friends, the Lord restored twice as much to Job as he had before. This followed a custom of the day which was to restore twice as much for damage inflicted on another. Job's brothers and sisters and his former acquaintances came to him and dined with him, a sign of renewed relationships. Each one gave him some money and a gold ring.

The Lord blessed the later days of Job more than the earlier ones. He had 14,000 sheep, 6,000 camels, 1,000 yoke of oxen, and 1,000 she-donkeys. He had seven sons and three beautiful daughters who received an inheritance with their brothers. The daughters' names were Jemimah (dove), Keziah (precious perfume), and Keren-happuch (cosmetic jar). Ordinarily, daughters did not receive an inheritance with their brothers unless they were the only children. The names of the daughters and the gesture of generosity emphasized the vast goodness of Job. He lived another 140 years and saw his offspring as far as his great-grandchildren, a glorious blessing for the people of Job's era. He died of old age after a full life.

Lectio Divina

Spend 8 to 10 minutes in silent contemplation of the following passage:

In the first speech of the book, Eliphaz tells Job to accept for himself what he taught others, namely blessings come for the good and suffering for the wicked. At the end of the book, Job learns a different lesson. The book tells us we cannot judge people's spiritual life by their success or failure in life. Jesus put blessings in perspective when he said, "Much will be required of the person entrusted with much, and still more will be demanded of the person entrusted with more" (Luke 12:48). The more prosperous we are, the greater our obligation to share with others.

✠ *What can I learn from this passage?*

Review Questions

1. What common theme is found in the speeches of Job's three friends?
2. What is Job's quandary?
3. How does the Lord treat Job?
4. What is Job's response to the Lord?

The Book of Psalms (I)

PSALMS 1–72

Indeed, goodness and mercy will pursue me all the days of my life; I will dwell in the house of the LORD for endless days (Psalm 23:6).

Opening Prayer (SEE PAGE 15)

Context

Part 1: Psalms 1—6 The Book of Psalms contains 150 psalms (songs) prayed either by an individual or a community. The psalms are a collection of five books of psalms joined as one in the Bible (1–41, 42–72, 73–89, 90–106, and 107–150). This lesson (3) includes the first two books of the psalms (1–41 and 42–72). Although these psalms are attributed to David, they were most likely not written by him.

Most of the psalms contain superscriptions, which are introductory remarks, giving directions to those who sing the psalm within a community liturgy or designating the author of the psalm. Although a number of the superscriptions identify a particular psalm as a psalm of David, this is not true in a large number of cases. Commentators are able to identify five books of psalms found in the Book of Psalms. Due to the large number of psalms, this commentary can only offer a short description of each psalm without treating each verse of the psalms in detail.

Psalm 1 serves as a preface for the whole book. Psalm 2 is a psalm for a royal coronation, and Psalms 3 to 6 deal with prayers of trust in God.

Part 2: Psalms 7—72 Although the Book of Psalms consists of five collections of psalms, most of the collections do not have a common theme, and the psalms in the collections are not connected to each other. The psalms must be considered independently of each other. Psalms 1–72 comprise books 1 and 2 of the Book of Psalms.

PART 1: GROUP STUDY (PSALMS 1—6)

Read aloud Psalms 1—6.

1—6 Help in Distress

Psalm 1 is a post-exilic wisdom psalm, presenting an overview of the message of the psalms and contrasting the life and rewards of the good with the life and punishment of the wicked. The faithful, who do not walk in the ways of the wicked or mix with sinners, will find joy in the Mosaic Law and flourish and prosper like a tree planted near streams that continually water it.

Psalm 2 is a royal psalm for a king's coronation or to be used on his anniversary of enthronement. The underlying theme of the psalms concerning kings is that the king should rule like a shepherd caring for his sheep. The king shall be king of all on earth, called to rule with an iron rod and shatter the wicked like a potter's vessel.

Psalm 3 is a lament by an individual who trusts God will save him, no matter how often his enemies may claim there is no salvation in God. The majority of the psalms are psalms of lament that may be either communal or individual psalms. The psalm of lament begins with an expression of the psalmist's or communities' sad situation and ends with a prayer of praise to God. The Lord protects faithful kings and people, bringing them help in their afflictions. The psalm teaches the people to trust God in the midst of affliction. The psalmist believes the Lord will answer his call and protect him, enabling him to sleep and wake in peace.

Psalm 4 is the lament of an individual who begs the Lord to have pity on him and hear his prayer. He speaks of the Lord as a saving God and laments over the hardness of hearts of the people who chase after worthless things. In contrast, the Lord works wonders for those who are faithful and hears their prayer. Those who put their trust in the Lord will lie down and fall asleep feeling secure.

Psalm 5 is an individual lament seeking the help of the Lord. It is a song of hope for those who trust the Lord. The Lord takes no delight in evil and will never grant refuge to those who are wicked. The psalmist speaks of bowing down in the Temple with a reverential fear of the Lord, seeking protection against one's enemy. The psalmist compares the throat of the wicked to an open grave, full of decay and spouting lies. He pleads with the Lord to allow their own treachery to destroy them.

Psalm 6 is a lament of an individual and the first of seven psalms known as penitential psalms because they convey true repentance. The penitential psalms are Psalms 6, 32, 38, 51, 102, 130, and 143. Suffering from an unknown offense against the Lord, the psalmist begs the Lord not to punish him but to show pity because he is weak. He believes the Lord has heard his prayer and all his enemies will be turned away in disgrace.

Review Questions

1. What is the message of Psalm 1?
2. How does trust in God help the psalmist in Psalm 4?
3. What does Psalm 5 say about a person's relationship to God?

Closing Prayer (SEE PAGE 15)

Pray the closing prayer now or after *lectio divina.*

Lectio Divina (SEE PAGE 8)

Relax your body and maintain a posture of prayer (back straight, eyes shut, feet flat on the floor). This exercise can take as long as you want, but in the context of this Bible study, 10 to 20 minutes should be sufficient.

The meditations that follow are provided only to help group participants use this prayer form, but note that *lectio* is intended to bring one to a place of prayerful contemplation where the Word of God speaks to the hearer from his or her heart. (See page 8 for further instruction.)

Psalms 1—6

The psalmist writes that those who walk with trust in the Lord are like a tree planted near running water. A dominant message found in the first six psalms speaks of God's help for those who place their trust in the Lord. Those who trust in the Lord always find peace, no matter what happens to them.

✠ *What can I learn from this passage?*

PART 2: INDIVIDUAL STUDY (PSALMS 7—72)

Day 1: First Book of Psalms, Continued (Psalms 7—24)

Psalm 7 is an individual lament that offers encouragement to a person unjustly accused. Convinced he has not sinned, the psalmist asks the Lord to judge his righteousness and bring to an end the evil of the wicked. Referring to the Lord as a just and powerful judge, the psalmist speaks of the Lord as a shield, saving the just and attacking the unjust with sword and arrows. The psalmist ends by thanking the Lord for acting justly and commits himself to singing praise to the Lord, Most High.

Psalm 8 addresses the awesomeness of God and praises the dignity of human beings in creation. The psalmist speaks of the majesty of God over everything on earth. When the psalmist contemplates the vastness of the heavens created by the Lord and the place of the moon and stars, he wonders why the Lord is so mindful of human beings whom the Lord has made "little less than a god" and crowned with glory and honor.

Psalms 9 and 10 are thanksgiving psalms which, although listed as separate psalms in the Hebrew text, form a single psalm. Each verse of the psalms begins with a successive letter of the Hebrew alphabet. The use of this alphabetic approach is known as the "acrostic" style and is used in several psalms. The author's need to remain faithful to the successive letters of the Hebrew alphabet often leads to difficulty in translating a particular psalm using this style. Because of this, translations of such a psalm may differ from other translations of the same psalm due to the need for the translator to guess the meaning of some words within the psalm.

The thanksgiving psalm first states the dire situation of the author and ends with the Lord answering the psalmist's plea for help. The specific dire situation is not always clearly identified. The psalmist calls upon the nations to sing songs of praise to the Lord, who is enthroned in Zion. He calls upon the Lord to rise and judge the nations, striking the enemy with terror and thus showing them they are mere human beings, unable to fight against the Lord. He states the wicked believe they will never meet with misfortune. The psalmist believes the Lord defends the helpless and orphans.

Psalm 11 is a prayer of trust by an individual who has confidence in the presence of the Lord. Although many flee to the mountains for refuge against the enemy, the psalmist takes refuge in the Lord. The psalmist views the punishment of the wicked as their "allotted cup," which means they must drink of the cup of wrath they themselves filled with their sins. The just God loves just deeds, and the upright will see the face of the Lord.

Psalm 12 is a lament bemoaning the absence of the faithful who have vanished from among the people, leaving only those who lie and speak deceptively. He pictures the Lord as promising to rise up against those who rob the weak and the needy, while granting security to the just who long for it. The Lord protects the people from the wicked who roam on every side and receive praise from those who favor their evil ways.

Psalm 13 is an individual lament in which the psalmist feels he has been abandoned by the Lord. He asks how long the Lord's face will remain hidden, how long he must remain sorrowful, and how long his enemy will prevail over him. Lest the enemy rejoice at his destruction, he begs the Lord to help him to avoid death. The psalmist begs the Lord to grant him the joy of salvation, and he sings to the Lord who has blessed him with abundance.

Psalm 14 is an individual lament that contrasts the deeds of the foolish with those of the wise who trust God. The message found in Psalm 14 is identical to Psalm 53 with few exceptions. The psalmist writes that the foolish perform hateful and corrupt deeds, rejecting the existence of God. The aim of the wicked is to "crush the hopes of the poor," but the poor have the Lord as their protector. The psalmist prays for salvation to come from Zion (Jerusalem).

Psalm 15 is a liturgical hymn used to examine the worthiness of those entering the tent of the Lord. Some of the psalms were sung in community and others were songs of individual psalmists. A song of praise may also be the song of an individual offering thanks to God. This psalm is similar to Psalm 24. The people who enter the Lord's Temple must be blameless, just, and truthful, avoiding all slander, evil deeds, and false accusations. They must not charge interest on a loan and refuse to accept a bribe against the innocent.

Psalm 16 professes trust in the Lord. The Lord delights in the holy ones in the land. The wicked, however, cause their own punishment by seeking other gods. The Lord refuses to speak their name, a sign of their rejection by the Lord. The psalmist speaks of "my allotted portion and my cup" bringing him security. The reference to the "allotted portion" refers to the portion of the land given to the psalmist that would be passed on to his offspring. The Lord will bless the godly one with a long life.

Psalm 17 is a lament of a person unjustly attacked. The psalmist prays with confidence for justice, knowing the Lord, who sees what is right, has justified him. He calls upon the Lord to slay the enemy with the sword, killing them in their youth. The oppressors fatten themselves with the plunder and life of the Lord's friends (the Israelites) and share their conquests with their children. The psalmist ends with a note of triumph, asking to see the Lord's face and, upon waking from all this evil, to experience the presence of the Lord.

Psalm 18 is a royal psalm of thanksgiving for victory over an enemy. The psalm repeats with few exceptions the song of David found in 2 Samuel 22, sung after the Lord freed him from the hands of Saul and those oppressing him.

The psalmist uses cosmic images to describe the response of the Lord to David's prayer. The heavens opened and the Lord emerged in the midst of a dark cloud, mounted on a cherub (a mythical winged creature), carried along on the wings of the wind, cloaked in darkness, and covered with storm clouds as a canopy. When the enemy cried for help to the Lord, they received no answer. In the midst of all the nations, David praised the Lord, who anointed him as king and promised victory and mercy for him and his descendants.

Psalm 19 praises God as the creator of the heavens and views the days and nights as silently offering praise to the Lord. In the midst of the firmament, the Lord set up a tent for the sun that arises like a bridegroom from his canopy and joyfully runs its course across the heavens. After praising God's creation, the psalmist praises the law of the Lord, declaring it to be perfect and bringing refreshment to one's soul. Without the law, who would know what is sinful. In following the law, the psalmist will live without blame and sin.

Psalm 20 is a liturgical prayer for a king's triumph in battle. The people pray the Lord will answer the prayer of the king and defend him. Some kings trust in chariots and others in horses, but chariots and horses collapse and fall. The Israelites place their trust in the Lord, who gives them the strength to remain firm.

Psalm 21 is a liturgical hymn following the same theme of victory for the king as Psalm 20. The Lord blessed the king and placed a crown of pure gold on his head. When the king asked for life, the Lord gave him a long life. The people believe the Lord fought on their side and are certain the Lord will find all the king's enemies and consume them and their descendants with fire. The people will sing and chant praise for the power of the Lord over their enemies.

Psalm 22 begins with a lament and ends with praise of God who delivered the people from oppression. The opening lament (22:2) recalls for Christians the words of Jesus on the cross: "My God, my God, why have you forsaken me?" (Mark 15:34). Later in the psalm, the people cry out against the psalmist, as those persecuting Jesus did, saying he trusted in the Lord, so let the Lord deliver him. The psalmist writes about the suffering he must endure, a passage spiritual writers applied to Jesus: "They have pierced my hands and my feet, I can count all my bones" (22:17b–18a). This is followed by a passage referred to in all the Gospels: "...They divide my garments among them; for my clothing they cast lots" (22:19) (see Matthew 27:35; Mark 15:24; Luke 23:34; John 19:24). Commentators believe Jesus prayed this psalm on the cross not only to express his feeling of abandonment, but also to show that no matter the oppression, God delivers his people. Generations to come will learn about the salvation the Lord brings.

Psalm 23, one of the most well-known and favored psalms, is a psalm of trust in the Lord who leads the people. Even under the shadow of death, the psalmist will experience no fear, knowing the shepherd (the Lord) is with him. The shepherd's rod and staff, used by the shepherd to guide the sheep, bring comfort to the trusting sheep. The psalmist shares in the Lord's table, a place of honor and friendship. The Lord anoints the psalmist's head with oil, a gesture of welcome and honor for guests at a banquet. The goodness and mercy of the Lord will be with the psalmist every day of his life. He vows to dwell in the house of the Lord (the Temple) for all his days.

Psalm 24 is a processional hymn used when entering the Temple. The psalm appears to be a liturgical ceremony with the people following the Ark of the Covenant into the Temple to enthrone it in the holy of holies. Those with clean hands and a pure heart, who reject all that is vain, may join the assembly in the Temple. The psalmist pictures the gates of Jerusalem as welcoming the Lord of hosts, opening up for the procession.

Lectio Divina

Spend 8 to 10 minutes in silent contemplation of the following passage:

The psalmist writes in Psalm 23: "Even though I walk through the valley of the shadow of death, I will fear no evil, for you are with me." Many people say they find comfort in Psalm 23, even in the face of death.

✠ *What can I learn from this passage?*

Day 2: End of First Book of Psalms (Psalms 25—41)

Psalm 25 is an individual lament in acrostic style (see page 48). The psalm is loosely held together. The people of ancient times believed a nation's victory proved a nation's god was more powerful than the god of the defeated nation. The psalmist professes faith in the Lord, stating no one who remains faithful is disgraced, whereas the wicked who worship false gods will be disgraced. The psalmist asks the Lord to make him truthful and just, and to redeem the Israelites from all their distress.

Psalm 26 is an individual lament of a person falsely attacked. The psalmist begins by declaring his faithfulness to the Lord and inviting the Lord to test his integrity. He expresses his love for the Temple (the house of the Lord) and delights in the prayers of thanksgiving and the recounting of the Lord's marvelous deeds.

Psalm 27 is a psalm of trust in which the psalmist proclaims the Lord is his light and salvation, his life's refuge who frees him from all fear. He longs to dwell in the Temple of the Lord and believes he will experience the Lord's goodness while he lives.

Psalm 28 is an individual lament by the psalmist as he prays in the Lord's holy place, a reference to the holy of holies, the most sacred place in the Temple. He begs the Lord not to drag him off with the wicked and deceitful people. He praises the Lord as the strength and refuge of the Israelites, calling upon the Lord to save, bless, and pasture them forever.

Psalm 29 calls upon the "sons of God" to glorify the Lord and bow down before the Lord's holy Temple. The term "sons of God" is a reference to the heavenly court surrounding the Lord. The psalmist pictures the Lord as enthroned above the flood. The ancients believed God created a dome in the sky separating the waters above the dome from the waters below (see Genesis 1:6–8). Above the dome was the throne of God, established over calm water. Upon this throne, the Lord reigns as king forever.

Psalm 30 is an individual's thanksgiving psalm. The psalmist thanks the Lord for answering his prayer by saving him from his enemies and lifting him up from the clutches of death to life. Fearing the Lord will kill him, he asks the Lord what profit there is in sending him into the grave. It was a common belief in ancient times that those who died could neither praise God nor sin against God. When the Lord responds to his prayer, the psalmist praises the Lord for changing his mourning into dancing. He promises to use his newfound glory to praise and thank the Lord forever.

Psalm 31 is an individual lament and a prayer thanking the Lord for delivering the psalmist from his afflictions. He prays to the Lord, saying, "Into your hands I commend my spirit" (v. 6). In Luke's Gospel, Jesus prays these words as he dies (see Luke 23:46). Knowing his destiny is in the Lord's hands, he begs the Lord to look favorably on him and save him while silencing the wicked in death. The Lord is the hope of the faithful.

Psalm 32, the second of the seven penitential psalms, is a thanksgiving psalm. The psalmist declares those whose sins are forgiven are blessed. Because the Lord, his shelter, guards him, the flood waters of his distress will never overwhelm him. He instructs the Israelites not to be like a stubborn mule that is controlled by a bit and bridle, and urges the righteous to rejoice and exult in the Lord.

Psalm 33 is a psalm of praise for the Lord, the creator and sustainer of the world. The Lord's word created the heavens with all their host (the stars) and gathered the waters of the sea within its boundaries. In the first story of creation, the author tells us the word of the Lord created the world, beginning each part of creation with the expression, "Then God said" (see Genesis 1:1–31). The psalmist notes the powerful army of a king is useless in the eye of the Lord.

Psalm 34 is a psalm of thanksgiving written in the acrostic style. The psalmist invites the humble to joyfully join him in exalting the Lord. The psalmist invites the people to taste and see the goodness of the Lord. The afflictions of the righteous are many, but the Lord delivers them, not allowing any of their bones to be broken. Evil brings death to the wicked, and those who hate the righteous will be condemned.

Psalm 35 is a psalm of lament by an individual betrayed by his friends. Viewing the Lord as his salvation, he begs the Lord to defeat those who plot evil against him. Despite his goodness to those he loved as a family member, they rejoiced when he stumbled and slandered him unceasingly. He begs the Lord to shame those who say they have destroyed him. He also prays the Lord to permit those who favor his just cause to shout out in joy and praise the Lord.

Psalm 36 is an individual lament by a person who is the victim of persecution yet remains loyal to the covenant. The psalmist speaks of the foolishness of the wicked person who believes God does not see his guilt. The psalmist praises the immense mercy, fidelity, justice, and judgments of the Lord, who provides refuge for the people in time of turmoil. After describing the blessings of the faithful, he prays the wicked will not overtake him, asking the Lord to destroy the evildoers.

Psalm 37 is a wisdom psalm in the acrostic style. The psalm presents short statements more like a list of wisdom sayings that answer the question, "Why do the wicked prosper and the good suffer?" The reader will notice similarities between the sayings in this psalm and the Beatitudes found in the Gospels (see Matthew 5:3–12). The Israelites are to trust the Lord and perform good works so they can dwell securely and happily in the land (the Promised Land). The Lord knows the heritage of the righteous will last forever, and they will have their fill in times of famine and will inherit the earth.

Psalm 38 is the third penitential psalm and a lament of one who is ill, sinful, and badly treated. He laments his physical and mental situation. He has foul and festering sores, is badly stooped, grieving day after day, wailing with an anguished heart, nearly blind, and abandoned by friends and neighbors. He grieves over his guilt and sinfulness while his enemies grow strong and numerous, repaying evil for good. The psalmist prays the Lord will not forsake him and will come quickly to help him.

Psalm 39 is the lament of a seriously ill and wasting-away individual. He is skeptical about life, viewing human beings as phantoms hurrying about in vain, storing up provisions without knowing who will use them. Recognizing the Lord as his only hope, the psalmist begs for deliverance from his sins and his enemies. He pleads with the Lord to allow him to smile before he leaves this life.

Psalm 40 is an individual lament and a thanksgiving psalm. The psalmist offers a prayer of thanksgiving to the Lord for hearing his plea and drawing him out of a muddy pit of destruction and placing him on a solid rock. In the Temple, he sings about the loyalty, salvation, mercy, and faithfulness of the Lord. He then addresses his weakness and lack of courage, being overwhelmed by his countless sins, more numerous than the hairs on his head, and he begs the Lord to come quickly and save him, shaming and destroying those who seek to ruin or kill him.

Psalm 41 is an individual's thanksgiving by the psalmist who recovers from an illness. The Lord cares for him with tenderness equal to someone turning down his bedding to comfort him. His trusted friend, who shared bread with him, has raised his heel against him, an insulting gesture of disrespect. The text recalls for Christians the Last Supper when Judas shares bread with Jesus. The psalmist seeks the help of the Lord, asking the Lord to raise him up so he may repay those who afflict him. The psalm concludes with a doxology. This ends the first collection of the Davidic psalms (Psalms 3–41).

Lectio Divina

Spend 8 to 10 minutes in silent contemplation of the following passage:

In Psalm 27:13, the psalmist writes: "I believe I shall see the LORD's goodness in the land of the living." The saints had the ability to see the presence of God in all of creation. In the Beatitudes in the Gospel of Matthew, Jesus said, "Blessed are the clean of heart, for they will see God" (Matthew 5:8).

✠ *What can I learn from this passage?*

Day 3: Beginning of Second Book of Psalms (Psalms 42—51)

Psalms 42 and 43 were originally a single psalm, demonstrated by an identical refrain linking 42:6 and 42:12 with 43:5. The psalms consist of an individual's lament. The psalmist longs to be in the Lord's presence with a yearning as strong as the yearning of a thirsty deer seeking water. He misses the day when he could enter the Temple, singing songs of thanksgiving with the community at festivals. He adds a refrain about hoping in the Lord and praising the Lord, who is his savior and God. His foes continue to ask him where his God is, and his inability to answer them cuts him to the bone. He ends this stanza with the refrain used at the end of the first stanza, hoping in the Lord and praising the Lord, who is his savior and God.

In Psalm 43, the psalmist's prayer becomes bolder as he begs the Lord for light to lead him to the holy mountain of Jerusalem, the altar of the Lord, where he will praise the Lord with the harp. He ends the psalm with the same refrain found in Psalm 42:6, 12, lamenting his desolation, yet hoping in the Lord and praising the Lord, who is his savior and God.

Psalm 44, a lament of a community, recalls the stories of the Lord's favor shown to their ancestors in rooting out nations to plant them in the Promised Land. They acknowledge the victories of their ancestors did not come with the arms of battle, but with the arm of the Lord. The community, however, now wonders why the Lord has abandoned them, handing them over to the enemy like sheep to be slaughtered. Despite their faithfulness and loyalty to the covenant, the Lord allows them to be crushed. They have been humiliated, crawling on their bellies in the dust. In a final plea, they ask the Lord to rise up and to mercifully help them.

Psalm 45 is a psalm for a royal wedding between a Davidic king and a foreign princess. The psalmist praises the attributes of the king, who is handsome, gracious in speech, and a great warrior who seeks truth, meekness, and justice. Since the Lord is the true king of Israel, the king of the nation, as a visible representative of the Lord, is viewed as more than human. The psalmist instructs the king's new wife to forget her people and her homeland because she now belongs to the king and is adorned as his queen. The king's name shall last forever. This does not refer to an individual king, but to the line of David.

Psalm 46 addresses God's presence in the Temple protecting the people. The psalmist speaks of a river bringing joy to the city of God, Jerusalem. Although no river runs through Jerusalem, the city where the Lord dwells brings refreshment no matter how disruptive the chaos. God dwells in the holy city, providing a place of refuge for the people. The psalmist calls the people to witness the works of the Lord who ends all wars and who proclaims a place of exaltation over all people. The Lord is their fortress.

Psalm 47 speaks of the Lord as the ruler of all nations. The psalmist proclaims the Lord as king of all the earth, not only over Israel. The psalm appears to be a liturgical enthronement ritual of the Lord of Israel, which includes joyful songs of praise. The princes of the nations join the Israelites in praising God.

Psalm 48 praises the city of Jerusalem, the city of God. The psalmist praises the Lord who is present in the city of God, which is the Lord's holy mountain, the city of the great king. The kings of other nations flee in fear before the Lord and the people of Judah rejoice in the power and just judgments of the Lord. The psalmist bids the people to walk around Zion and marvel at its towers and to pass the word of God's strength onto future generations.

Psalm 49 speaks of the futility of wealth's passing. The psalmist declares wealth cannot buy anyone back from the grave. When the wise and the foolish die, they leave their wealth to others. Those who trust only in themselves will die, while God will save the just. All wealth and glory will not go into the grave with the rich and foolish.

Psalm 50 explains true worship of God. The psalmist declares the Lord does not really need all their sacrifices, since all animals on earth belong to the Lord. If the people offer praise as their sacrifice and loyalty to the vows of the covenant, then the Lord will rescue them. The Lord rejects those who forget God and promises to bring salvation to those who offer a sacrifice of praise.

Psalm 51 is a lament of an individual who seeks the Lord's mercy. It is the fourth and best known of the penitential psalms. The psalmist begs the Lord to cleanse him of his sinfulness and make him whiter than snow. Knowing the Lord desires a contrite heart as a sacrifice rather than burnt offerings without a repentant heart, he begs the Lord to create a clean heart in him so he may teach the ways of the Lord to the wicked. He begs the Lord to restore Jerusalem so true burnt sacrifices may be offered.

Lectio Divina

Spend 8 to 10 minutes in silent contemplation of the following passage:

In Psalm 49:11, the psalmist reminds us of the foolishness of some wealthy people who spend their life gaining wealth, only to leave it to someone else when they die. The psalmist writes: "Indeed, he will see that the wise die, and the fool will perish together with the senseless, and they leave their wealth to others." Wealth is not gained to take with us in death but gained to share with others in life.

✠ *What can I learn from this passage?*

Day 4: Second Book of Psalms, Continued (Psalms 52—61)

Psalm 52 is an individual lament in which the psalmist asks the evil person whom the Lord makes mighty why he loves evil more than good. The Lord will destroy the wicked and protect the righteous. The psalmist rejoices that the righteous flourish, like an olive tree in the house of God.

Psalm 53, similar to Psalm 14, is a lament over foolish corruption. The psalmist notes those who are foolish perform hateful and corrupt deeds, rejecting the existence of God. The Lord searches for even one who is wise enough to seek God, but the people have gone astray, with no one found to do what is good. The Lord will scatter their bones, leaving them disgraced before all the nations. The psalmist prays for the salvation of Israel to come from Zion (Jerusalem).

Psalm 54, a lament, pleads for the Lord's help. The psalmist promises to offer a generous sacrifice to the Lord, if the Lord—who sustains him— turns the evil intended by the wicked back on them and destroys them. With the Lord's help, he will look down on his enemy.

Psalm 55 is an individual lament over betrayal by a close friend. The psalmist prays for the Lord, enthroned forever, to protect him and send his enemies into the Sheol, the place of the dead. His friend broke the covenant, using smooth words that aim to kill rather than help. He urges his friend to trust the Lord, who will save the righteous and bring evil liars into the grave.

Psalm 56, an individual's lament, demonstrates the psalmist's trust in the Lord. The psalmist explains his dire situation, surrounded by foes who seek to kill him. They turn away, however, when they witness the psalmist's trust in the Lord. He promises to fulfill the vows he made to the Lord, who keeps him alive.

Psalm 57 is an individual lament that begins with a description of the turmoil surrounding the psalmist and ends with a prayer of thanksgiving. The psalmist begs the Lord to rescue him and hide him in the shadow of the Lord's wings, an apparent reference to the Temple, considered a place of asylum for refugees. The wings may also refer to the wings of the images of the cherubim on each side of the Ark of the Covenant. At dawn (Morning Prayer), the psalmist will praise the Lord on the lyre and harp among the people. He pleads for the glory of God to appear over all the earth.

Psalm 58 is a lament concerning the punishment of unjust rulers. The psalmist speaks of the wicked as being corrupt from the womb, with venom like that of a serpent that closes its ears to the charmer who usually controls it. He prays for God to smash the foe's fangs or to make the enemy vanish as though caught in running waters. The just will rejoice in the Lord.

Psalm 59 is an individual lament against the wicked. The psalmist makes use of a refrain, "you, God, are my fortress, my loving God." He prays for the Lord to destroy his foes who deceive the people with their lies, swearing an oath each time they lie. The psalmist praises the Lord, ending with the refrain found earlier in this psalm, "you, God, are my fortress, my loving God."

Psalm 60 is a nation's lament after a defeat in battle. In the first stanza, the Israelites lament the Lord's rejection of them, causing hardship for them. They beg the Lord to help them triumph over the enemy, aware that human help is worthless.

Psalm 61 is a lament of a king nearing death. The king calls out from the depths of the earth for the Lord, his refuge, to lift him up to the Lord's tent where he will find shelter under the Lord's wings. He will praise the name of the Lord forever and fulfill his vows each day.

Lectio Divina

Spend 8 to 10 minutes in silent contemplation of the following passage:

> The psalmist writes: "Listen, God, to my prayer; do not hide from my pleading; hear me and give answer" (Psalm 55:2–3). Some people think they ask God for too much, but the reality is God made us people who need help. God wants us to ask for help. Jesus tells us, "Ask and it will be given to you" (Matthew 7:7).

✠ *What can I learn from this passage?*

Day 5: End of Second Book of Psalms (Psalms 62—72)

Psalm 62 is a psalm of trust in God. The psalmist extols the Lord as his rock, salvation, and refuge and calls upon others to trust the Lord. The people are not to put their trust in wealth, but in the Lord who pays people according to their deeds.

Psalm 63 expresses a close, intimate relationship between the worshiper and God. He desires to see the Lord, enthroned with power and glory, in the sanctuary (Temple). The intense love of the psalmist for the Lord shows itself in the psalmist's declaration he will bless the Lord as long as he lives. **Psalm 64** is an individual lament concerning the treachery of the enemy and God's punishment. The wicked plot evil against the psalmist. The psalmist declares God will kill his foes, whose own tongues betray them and force all who support them to flee.

Psalm 65 is a prayer of thanksgiving and petition. The one chosen to dwell in the house of the Lord receives an abundance of blessings. The psalmist extols the goodness and power of the Lord, stressing the awesome deeds of the Lord in creation. The Lord provides the much-needed rain for a bountiful harvest, providing food for animals and lush valleys of grain for people.

Psalm 66 is a prayer of thanksgiving and praise. The community recalls the awesome deeds of the Lord in opening up a dry path through the Red Sea so the Israelites could cross when fleeing from Egypt (see Exodus 14:19–22), and later, under Joshua, opening up a dry path through the Jordan so the Israelites could enter the Promised Land (see Joshua 3:14–17). Later in history, the Lord tested the Israelites as silver is tested when foreign conquerors ravaged them with fire and water.

Psalm 67 is a harvest song in praise of God. The refrain, "May the peoples praise you, God, may all the peoples praise you!" is repeated at the end of the first and second stanzas. The psalmist bids all nations to joyfully praise God, who is a fair judge and guide for the people. The psalm ends with a proclamation of praise similar to that at the end of the first and second stanzas.

Psalm 68 is a difficult psalm for translators since it is badly preserved and appears to be a collection of segments of ancient psalms referring to an uncertain ceremony. The psalmist recalls the time when God freed the Israelites from the grip of the Egyptians and led them to Sinai, where Moses received his visitations from God. God brought them to settle in the land of Canaan (the Promised Land). The psalmist describes a procession into God's Temple and calls all the nations to praise the mighty Lord, who protects Israel and who dwells in the holy place.

Psalm 69 is an individual's lament of anguish. In the first stanza, the psalmist likens his situation to a person immersed in water up to his neck, a symbol of his anguish and of chaos. Being insulted because of his zeal for the Lord, he prays his situation will not be the occasion of shame for others who seek the Lord. The psalmist curses his enemy, asking the Lord to reject their sacrifices and afflict them with poor eyesight, feeble backs, empty camps, and death. He speaks of the restoration of Zion and the cities of Judah, where those who love the Lord will dwell.

Psalm 70 is an individual lament, begging the Lord to save the psalmist from those who seek to kill him. He prays those who are faithful will find help from the Lord, the deliverer of the Israelites.

Psalm 71 is an elderly person's lament. He begs the Lord not to abandon him in his old age, at a time when others are plotting against him, believing no one will help him. He seeks to live so he may continue to praise the Lord, who has accomplished marvelous deeds and saved him from chaos.

Psalm 72 is a prayer for the king, but most likely not a psalm of Solomon as found in the superscription. The first stanza prays for an ideal king who governs justly, defends the oppressed, saves the children of the poor, crushes the oppressor, and brings an abundance of blessings upon the Israelites. He will protect the poor and oppressed from extortion and violence. A doxology, added by a later editor (verses 18 to 20) and a declaration saying this psalm ends the psalms of David, ends this second collection of psalms.

Lectio Divina

Spend 8 to 10 minutes in silent contemplation of the following passage:

Nothing satisfies us more than loving God. The psalmist grasped this well when he wrote: "O God, you are my God—it is you I seek! For you my body yearns; for you my soul thirsts" (Psalm 63:2). Those who long with love for God seem to exude joy in all they do.

✠ *What can I learn from this passage?*

Review Questions

1. What makes Psalm 23 so popular?
2. What does Psalm 42 say about longing for God?
3. Why do only some of the psalms have doxologies at the end?

The Book of Psalms (II)

PSALMS 73–150

LORD, hear my prayer; let my cry come to you. Do not hide your face from me in the day of my distress. Turn your ear to me, when I call, answer me quickly (Psalm 102:2–3).

Opening Prayer (SEE PAGE 15)

Context

Part 1: Psalms 73—76 Psalm 73 begins the third book of Psalms (73—89). The history of the Israelites is one of destruction and triumph, with the Lord always the center of what is happening to the people. Psalms 73 to 76 touch upon the trials of the people and their confusion when the Temple is destroyed. God, however, becomes their protector just when they think God has abandoned them.

Part 2: Psalms 77—150 These psalms explore the confidence the people have in God as their protector, their longing to remain faithful to the Lord in times of turmoil, their liturgical forms of worship, and their desire to offer continual praise to God. As well as continuing with the remainder of the third book of Psalms, this section includes the fourth and fifth book of Psalms (90—106 and 107—150).

PART 1: GROUP STUDY (PSALMS 73—76)

Read aloud Psalms 73—76.

Psalms 73—74 Beginning of Third Book of the Book of Psalms

Psalm 73 begins the third book of the Psalms (73—89). The psalm offers a prayer of praise for God, who is good to the just. The psalmist is confused over the pain he endures, despite his avoidance of evil, while the arrogant prosper. He finds comfort and protection in God, and he recognizes he is foolish not to realize the wicked only appear to flourish.

Psalm 74 is a community lament over the destruction of the Temple. The community begs the Lord to inform them how long God will abandon them. They recall the power of God which provided for them in the past and beg the Lord to arise and silence the enemy.

Psalms 75—76 Confidence in God

Psalm 75 is a psalm of thanksgiving and joy, possibly a liturgical hymn. The psalmist thanks the Lord for judging justly. Since judgment comes from God, whose wrath will pour out like wine on the wicked, the psalmist advises the wicked not to boast. In the meanwhile, the just will sing praises to the God of Israel.

Psalm 76 is a hymn praising Zion, the mountain of Jerusalem. The psalmist praises God's tent (the Temple) on Zion and praises God, who will judge and destroy the wicked. He speaks of the princes and kings of nations bringing gifts to God.

Review Questions

1. What does the psalmist think of pride and arrogance in Psalm 73?
2. Why does the psalmist feel a need to remind God about the favors the Lord once bestowed on the Israelites in Psalm 74?
3. What is the meaning of the image of the cup in the Lord's hand in Psalm 75?

Closing Prayer (SEE PAGE 15)

Pray the closing prayer now or after *lectio divina*.

Lectio Divina (SEE PAGE 8)

Relax your body and maintain a posture of prayer (back straight, eyes shut, feet flat on the floor). This exercise can take as long as you want, but in the context of this Bible study, 10 to 20 minutes should be sufficient.

The meditations that follow are provided only to help group participants use this prayer form, but note that *lectio* is intended to bring one to a place of prayerful contemplation where the Word of God speaks to the hearer from his or her heart. (See page 8 for further instruction.)

Trusting God in Turmoil (Psalms 73—74)

The psalmist in Psalm 73 wonders why the arrogant seem to prosper until he realizes they miss what is truly fulfilling in life, namely knowing, loving, and serving God. He rejects the empty glory of the wicked and writes in verse 28: "As for me, to be near God is my good, to make the Lord God my refuge."

✠ *What can I learn from this passage?*

God Is With the Just (Psalms 75—76)

In Psalm 75, the psalmist realizes true judgment does not come from the world but from God who knows all. What matters is what God thinks, not what the world thinks. The psalmist writes: "For judgment comes not from east or from west, not from the wilderness or the mountains, but from God who decides, who brings some low and raises others high" (75:7–8).

✠ *What can I learn from this passage?*

PART 2: INDIVIDUAL STUDY (PSALMS 77—150)

Day 1: Third Book of Psalms, Continued (Psalms 77—89)

Psalm 77 is an individual lament on behalf of the community. The psalmist fears God has abandoned the community. He recalls the wondrous deeds of the mighty Lord, who led the Israelites through the mighty waters (the Red Sea) under the leadership of Moses and Aaron.

Psalm 78 seeks to teach the Israelites a lesson from their own history. God split the Red Sea, allowing the Israelites to cross. In the desert, God provided water, bread, and meat for them, but when they demanded more, God became angry and sent a curse upon them, killing many of their young men. The Lord afflicted the Egyptians by turning the rivers to blood, overwhelming the land with insects, frogs, and locusts, and killing the firstborn of animals and Egyptians. The Lord led the people out of slavery, through the wilderness to the holy mountain (Mount Zion). The Lord selected the tribe of Judah (the southern kingdom) over Joseph and Ephraim (the northern kingdom) and chose Mount Zion for the Temple and the Davidic kingship to shepherd the people.

Psalm 79 is a lament of the community over the destruction of the Temple. The psalmist laments the shame the Israelites face in the eyes of the nations and the dire conditions in Jerusalem, with the Temple and city destroyed and corpses left unburied. The psalmist prays for help to show the nations the existence and power of the God of Israel.

Psalm 80 is a community lament over the destruction of the Israelite nation. The psalmist speaks of the Lord bringing a vine (the Israelites) out of Egypt and driving the nations from the land so the Israelites could flourish, but now the Lord is leaving them unprotected and ravaged. They promise to remain faithful if the Lord will save them and protect the Davidic king.

Psalm 81 is a psalm used for a liturgical feast, possibly the feast of Tabernacles. The people celebrate with the lyre and harp on the occasion of the full moon, a harvest feast, in accord with the Law of the Lord (see Leviticus 23:23–25). The Lord repeats the First Commandment warning against worship of a foreign god and the need to worship the one true God (see Exodus 20:1–2). The Lord is willing to satisfy their needs if only they would heed the words of the Lord.

Psalm 82 pictures the Lord in the midst of a heavenly assembly judging the "gods." In this instance, the reference to gods means angels and others who belong to the heavenly court. The Lord asks the gods how long they will support the wicked and commands them to defend the lowly, fatherless, afflicted, and needy. God condemns the gods who, like mortals or earthly princes, will wander in darkness and will die.

Psalm 83 is a community lament against destructive alliances. Nations were joining together to invade the land of the Israelites. The psalmist names the occasions in the past when the Lord punished people for their sins (see Judges 4—8) and asks the Lord to deal with their enemies in the same manner.

Psalm 84 is a psalm of praise by people eager to enter the Temple. The psalmist praises the dwelling place of the Lord and yearns to enter into the courts of the Temple. He says one day in the Temple is better than a thousand elsewhere. The one who trusts in the Lord is blessed by the Lord.

Psalm 85 is a national lament. The psalmist recalls the favors the Lord bestowed on the land and the captives who returned from exile. He begs the Lord not to remain angry with the community and prays the Lord will restore their life and grant them salvation. Surely, the Lord will grant them love and truth, justice and peace, and a bountiful harvest.

Psalm 86 is an individual lament. The psalmist praises God, believing all nations will praise the God of Israel, who performs marvelous deeds. He continues to praise the merciful Lord for keeping him from death (Sheol). The arrogant seek his life, paying no attention to God who is filled with mercy and truth. He prays the Lord will allow the nations to see how the Lord favors him.

Psalm 87 is a song of Zion. The psalmist speaks of God's great love for Zion, the holy mountain. He names nations where the Israelites lived in exile and declares the Israelites belonged to Zion, no matter where they were born or lived.

Psalm 88 is an individual lament for a person near death. The psalmist, who believes the Lord is angry with him as he nears his death, calls upon the Lord to hear his prayer. The images used for death include Sheol, the pit, the dead, the slain, the grave, and the abyss. Because his friends and neighbors surge around him like a flood, he believes his only friend is darkness.

Psalm 89 is a communal lamentation of the Davidic dynasty. The Lord promised David his dynasty would last forever. Justice and judgment are the foundations of the throne of the mighty Lord, who is the shield of the people, the Holy One of Israel, the true king. The Lord exalts David as the anointed leader of the people. A later editor of the text added a song of praise to the Lord (89:53), which is not part of Psalm 89, to mark the end of the third book of the Psalms.

Lectio Divina

Spend 8 to 10 minutes in silent contemplation of the following passage:

> The psalmist in Psalm 88 demonstrates an example of the need to pray in times of turmoil when he writes: "Lord, the God of my salvation, I call out by day; at night I cry aloud in your presence. Let my prayer come before you; incline your ear to my cry" (88:2–3). Our prayers should be constant and prayers of trust in God.

✠ *What can I learn from this passage?*

Day 2: Fourth Book of Psalms (Psalms 90—106)

Psalm 90 begins the fourth book of psalms and is a communal lament describing the community's suffering. The psalmist addresses the eternal Lord as the refuge of the people of the community. He begs the Lord to teach the people to live wisely and prays for the Lord to bless the people with as many days of joy equal to the number of days they suffered.

Psalm 91 is a song of refuge. The psalmist speaks to those who take refuge in the Lord in the Temple. The Lord will shelter the people so they need not fear the terror of the night, the arrow that flies during the day (war), pestilence, plague, or the slaughter of battle. The Lord will protect them with honor and a long life.

Psalm 92 is a hymn of thanksgiving for God's faithfulness. The psalmist praises the love and faithfulness of the Lord on the harp and lyre. The wicked may flourish like grass, but they are destined for eternal punishment. The psalmist claims he is flourishing like a palm tree, like a tree planted and prospering in the Temple, bearing fruit even when old, and praising the just Lord as his rock without blemish.

Psalm 93 praises the Lord as a mighty king, firmly enthroned and robed with majesty and a power greater than the roar of many waters and the breaking waves. The decrees of the Lord are firmly established and the Temple of the Lord is holy.

Psalm 94 is an individual lament, a prayer of deliverance from evil. The psalmist asks how long will the wicked boast about their sin, believing the Lord does not see them. He refers to the wicked as stupid people, asking if the one who shaped the ear could not hear, the one who shaped the eye not see, the one who guides nations not rebuke, and the one who teaches not have knowledge. He declares the one who is blessed will receive a just judgment while the wicked will fall into a pit.

Psalm 95 is a song of praise for the Lord. The psalmist invites the people to acknowledge the Lord as their shepherd. The Lord warns the people not to harden their hearts as in the days of testing in the desert. When the people sinned, the Lord declared they would not enter the Promised Land.

Psalm 96 is a psalm inviting all people to praise the glories of Israel's God. The psalmist declares the Lord is the king who rules all people with justice. He bids nature to join in the praise of the Lord, calling upon the heavens, the earth, the sea, the plains, and the trees of the forest to rejoice in the presence of the Lord who comes to govern the world and the people with justice and faithfulness.

Psalm 97 is an enthronement psalm stressing the preeminence of God. All creation—clouds and darkness, fire, lightning, and the volcanoes—proclaims the justice and glory of the Lord. The Lord protects those who act with love and rescues the faithful from the hand of the wicked.

Psalm 98 is an enthronement psalm similar to Psalm 96. The psalmist invites the people to sing a new song to the Lord, whose victories are seen by all the nations and who is merciful and faithful to the Israelites. The psalmist calls upon the sea, the world, and all that fills it—the rivers, and mountains—to praise the Lord who comes to govern the world with justice and fairness.

Psalm 99 is the last of the enthronement psalms. The psalmist invites all of creation to praise the great and awesome name of the Lord. He states that Moses and Aaron, priests of the Lord, and Samuel received an answer from the Lord, who spoke to them from a cloud. The psalmist praises the Lord for forgiving and punishing the people as they needed it.

Psalm 100 is a processional hymn of praise. The psalmist calls the people of all lands to praise the Lord with a joyful song. He proclaims the Lord is God who made us and invites the people to enter the Temple with prayers of thanks and blessings, proclaiming the Lord's goodness, mercy, and faithfulness.

Psalm 101 consists of a psalm from a king to the Lord. The king sings a song of mercy, promising to act with integrity, rejecting whatever is evil, refusing the company of the liar, the slanderer, and the arrogant. Each day he ejects the wicked from the city of the Lord.

Psalm 102 is the fifth of the penitential psalms and an individual lament of one who is seriously ill. His sufferings include fever and a weak heart, making him too weak to eat. He begs the Lord—who exists forever while the lives of the people wear out like a garment—to allow the children of Israel to live on in the Lord's presence.

Psalm 103 is an individual psalm of praise. The psalmist praises the Lord who is gracious, slow to anger, and does not punish people as their sins deserve. The Lord knows humans are dust whose existence is like a flower in the field which disappears. The psalmist bids all creation, including the angels, to bless the Lord, whose dominion extends over all.

Psalm 104 praises God for creating and sustaining the world. The psalmist blesses the splendor of the Lord in nature and prays sinners will disappear from the earth. He ends his psalm with an outburst of joy: "Hallelujah."

Psalm 105 is a poetic reflection on the history of the Israelites. The psalmist calls on the people to reflect on all the Lord did for the descendants of Abraham and Jacob by destroying their enemies. He speaks of Joseph bringing his family into Egypt, the escape from Egypt under the leadership of Moses and Aaron, the bread and meat given to the rebellious Israelites in the desert, and the gift of the Promised Land. The Lord gave them the wealth of the nations so they would remain faithful to the Law and teachings of the Lord: Hallelujah!

Psalm 106 is a communal lament that thanks the Lord, who blesses those who remain faithful. After the Israelites passed through the Red Sea on dry land under the leadership of Moses, the water flowed again, drowning the enemy's army. When the people challenged Moses and Aaron in the wilderness, the earth swallowed the leaders of the rebellion. At Horeb (Mount Sinai) the people chose to worship a statue of a calf in place of the God of Israel.

A grandson of Aaron, named Phinehas, killed a pagan woman and an Israelite man who brought the woman into his tent. His action ended a plague ravaging the people (see Numbers 25:6–9). God became angry with the people when they rebelled, demanding water to drink. The Lord told Moses to strike a rock and water poured out for the people to drink (see Exodus 17:1–7).

When the people finally entered the Promised Land and worshiped the foreign gods of the land, the Lord allowed their enemies to oppress them. The psalm ends with a doxology praising God (106:48), marking the end of the fourth collection of psalms.

Lectio Divina

Spend 8 to 10 minutes in silent contemplation of the following passage:

> In Psalm 104, the psalmist acknowledges God speaks to us not only through revelation but also through creation itself. The psalmist writes: "How varied are your works, LORD! In wisdom you have made them all; the earth is full of your creatures" (104:24). By contemplating God's creation, we can learn more about God.

✠ *What can I learn from this passage?*

_____

Day 3: Beginning of the Fifth Book of Psalms (Psalms 107—121)

Psalm 107 begins the fifth collection of psalms (Psalms 107—150) in the Book of Psalms. Some chose the darkness of rebellion against God, and God imposed hardship on them. They cried out to the Lord, who blessed the faithful with water and an abundant harvest.

Psalm 108 is a psalm of praise and prayer for victory. The psalmist prays for the Lord to help the community, noting the Lord possesses the land and is able to provide for the people as the Lord wishes. The psalmist declares only God, not human help, will enable the community to triumph.

Psalm 109 is an individual lament in which the author professes his need for God's help against those who slander and attack him, although he loved and prayed for them. Recounting the evil deeds of the wicked who oppressed and killed the poor and brokenhearted, he prays the wicked will suffer the curses they imposed on others. The psalmist prays for the wicked to recognize the hand of the Lord in his deliverance.

Psalm 110 is a royal psalm in honor of a Davidic king. The psalm begins: "The LORD says to my lord: 'Sit at my right hand, while I make your enemies your footstool.'" Jesus alludes to this first line when confronting the religious leaders of his day who claim the Messiah is a son of David (see Matthew 22:41–46). Fathers were considered to be greater than their offspring, yet David seems to be saying his offspring will be greater than he: "The LORD says to my lord..." In Psalm 110, the psalmist is referring to David as the one sitting at the right hand of God. In ancient times, the victorious king would make his enemies his footstool by placing his feet on their prostrate bodies. The Lord declares the Davidic king to be a priest forever in the order of Melchizedek. Kings were often considered to be priests in ancient times. Melchizedek was a kingly priest of Salem (Jerusalem) who blessed Abraham and went away. Since nothing is said of Melchizedek's death, his priesthood is considered to last forever (see Genesis 14:18–20).

Psalm 111 is a psalm of an individual who praises the Lord's glorious works in the presence of the community. The psalmist proclaims the Lord will provide food for those who are faithful and grant them the inheritance of the nation. The psalm ends by proclaiming fear of the Lord is the beginning of wisdom. The prudent are those who fear (revere) the Lord.

Psalm 112 is a psalm declaring the person who reveres and obeys the Lord's commands is blessed. The rewards of such reverence lead to powerful, just, and rich offspring. The righteous person will live in peace, without fear, and will dominate his foes. The wicked will waste away.

Psalm 113 bids the community to praise the name of the Lord both now and forever, "from the rising of the sun to its setting" (113:3). He praises the Lord who is enthroned high above the heavens, lifting up the needy from the dust and providing a home for the wife without children.

Psalm 114 speaks of the Israelites leaving Egypt and settling in Judah, God's sanctuary. The psalmist speaks poetically to nature, asking the sea (Reed Sea) and the Jordan why it turned back. The Lord turned a rock into water and flint into a spring, a reference to the time Moses struck the rock and water flowed from it (see Exodus 17:1–7).

Psalm 115 taunts those who worship idols for asking where the God of Israel is. The psalmist ridicules those who worship idols made of silver and gold with mouths unable to speak, eyes unable to see, ears unable to hear, noses unable to smell, hands unable to feel, feet unable to walk, and throats unable to speak. The psalmist declares the heavens belong to the Lord who has given the care of the earth to the children of Adam (humans).

Psalm 116 is a psalm of thanksgiving to God. The psalmist asserts the Lord, who is gracious and righteous, saved him when he was helpless and near death. He declares he will toast the Lord with the cup of salvation and remain faithful to the Lord. He offers a sacrifice of praise to the Lord, faithful to the vows he made before everyone in the Temple.

Psalm 117, the shortest psalm, calls upon all nations and peoples to praise the Lord. The psalmist extols the mercy and faithfulness of the Lord.

Psalm 118 is a thanksgiving liturgy of an individual speaking on behalf of the community. The psalmist writes: "The stone the builders rejected has become the cornerstone" (118:22). The passage appears to refer to the capstone of the Temple. In the New Testament, the verse is applied to the death and resurrection of Jesus Christ (see Matthew 21:42, Acts 4:11, and 1 Peter 2:7). The psalmist prays for the Lord to grant him good fortune and cries out, "Blessed is he who comes in the name of the LORD" (118:26). He invites the people to join in procession with leafy branches, an apparent reference to the feast of Tabernacles.

Psalm 119 is the longest psalm in the Book of Psalms. Its central theme is the love of the Lord's commands and the desire of the psalmist to change his life in accord with the law of the Lord. The psalmist prays to remain faithful to the Lord's commandments. By observing God's precepts, the young can keep the way of the Lord without fault. Begging the Lord to teach him the commandments, he prays he will not stray from these precepts that bring him joy. The arrogant envelop him with lies, but he remains faithful to the Lord's precepts with all his heart. Because his affliction led him to learn the Lord's statutes, he declares it was good for him to be afflicted. The law from the mouth of the Lord is more precious to him than mountains of silver and gold.

Due to his love for the law, the psalmist believes he is wiser than his foes and has gained more insight than all his teachers and the elders. He becomes enraged when the Lord's foes ignore the decrees of the Lord. Each day, he praises the Lord seven times. Claiming he once wandered like a lost sheep, he ends his long prayer by begging the Lord to remain with him as a result of his faithfulness to the law.

Psalm 120 begins with the superscription designating it as "a song of ascents," which could mean it is a song for pilgrimage to Jerusalem, since the Scriptures speak of "going up to Jerusalem" (1 Kings 12:28). Psalms 120 to 134 all begin with this superscription, which indicates these fifteen psalms formed a collection of psalms sung when pilgrims traveled to Jerusalem. The psalmist pleads with the Lord to deliver him from the deceitful enemy. He prays on behalf of the Israelites living in foreign lands far to the North (Meshech) and the South (Kedar) who find themselves among people who love war rather than peace.

Psalm 121 is a song of trust in God for one about to begin a journey. The traveler raises his eyes toward the mountains, a possible reference to Mount Zion, where the Lord dwells in the Temple. He believes the Lord will guide him safely on his journey. The Lord, who never sleeps, will be the traveler's guardian, providing shade against the sun and moon.

Lectio Divina

Spend 8 to 10 minutes in silent contemplation of the following passage:

In Psalm 108, the psalmist speaks of praising the Lord at the beginning of the day. "Awake, lyre and harp! I will wake the dawn. I will praise you among the peoples, LORD; I will chant your praise among the nations" (108:3–4). Each morning we can thank the Lord for blessing us with another day and another opportunity to make our day an offering to God.

✠ *What can I learn from this passage?*

Day 4: End of the Fifth Book of Psalms (Psalms 122—150)

Psalm 122 is a song of Zion, praising Jerusalem. The psalmist rejoiced when the people invited him to go to the house of the Lord, into the Lord's presence. In Jerusalem were the thrones of justice, which were the thrones the judges used in passing judgment (see 1 Kings 7:7). In Jerusalem, the people prayed for the peace and prosperity of Jerusalem, for the sake of the people and of the Temple.

Psalm 123 is a lament of an individual speaking for the community. Just as the eyes of servants are on their masters or the eyes of a maid on her mistress, so the eyes of the people are on the Lord God till the Lord favors them by answering their prayer. Because the community is filled with the mockery and contempt of the arrogant, the psalmist expresses the community's need for the Lord's help.

Psalm 124 is a prayer of thanksgiving by the community for the Lord's guidance and protection. The people in the community realize they would have been totally ravaged by their foes if the Lord had not been with them. They praise the Lord, who saved them from being torn to pieces.

Psalm 125 is a song of trust prayed by the community. Those who trust the Lord are like Mount Zion, which endures forever. Just as mountains surround Jerusalem, the Lord surrounds the Israelites, protecting them against the reign of the wicked. The Lord will perform good works for those who remain faithful and will punish the wicked.

Psalm 126 is a psalm of lament and thanksgiving. The Israelites will laugh with joy when they enter Jerusalem after their many years in exile. When other nations witness the return of the people from exile, they will realize the God of Israel performed wonderful marvels for the Israelites. The returning exiles declare the Lord has indeed done great things for them. They sow in tears and reap in joy, carrying an abundant harvest of sheaves.

Psalm 127 is a wisdom psalm using two proverbs to express the people's need to trust God rather than their own gifts in building their lives. It is foolish for someone to ignore God, thinking that rising early and sleeping less will accomplish all that needs to be done. The admiration for a father of many sons allows him to be accepted as a wise judge at the gate of the city, where judgment takes place.

Psalm 128 is a wisdom psalm teaching that trust in the Lord will provide stability in the family and community. The Lord will bless the man who fears the Lord and follows the Lord's precepts. His wife shall be like a fruitful vine within his home. Children shall be like young olive plants around the table. The psalmist prays the Lord will allow the faithful to live to see their children's children. Seeing children's children was a great blessing, which meant a person would live a long life.

Psalm 129 speaks of the oppression the Israelites had to endure, their eventual freedom obtained by the intervention of the Lord, and their prayer for a poor harvest for their oppressors. The Israelites endured the violent attacks of their foes, but their foes were unable to wipe their name from the earth. The enemy plowed through the Israelite community like a farmer plowing a field, but the Lord, like a farmer who cuts his ox free, will cut the Israelites free from the shackles of the wicked. The Israelites prayed for a retreat in disgrace of those who hate Zion.

Psalm 130, one of the penitential psalms, teaches about the Lord's forgiveness and mercy to the sinner. The psalmist prays the Lord will hear his cry for mercy. If the Lord holds his sins against him, he would find this hard to accept. He trusts in the forgiveness of the Lord and prays Israel will wait as patiently for the Lord as the sentinels wait for daybreak. He believes the Lord is merciful and will redeem Israel from its sins.

Psalm 131 is a simple psalm of trust in God, promising the people comfort from the Lord. The psalmist declares he is not proud or haughty, nor does he bother with things too sublime for his attention. Rather, he is content to rest, like a weaned child on its mother's lap. He calls upon Israel to hope in the Lord forever.

Psalm 132 is a royal psalm concerning the Davidic dynasty and the Temple. The psalmist calls upon God to remember when David swore he would not enter his house or sleep on his couch until he found a dwelling place for the Mighty One of Jacob (Israel). David was speaking of having a house (Temple) for the Ark of the Covenant. On top of the Ark were figures of two angels facing each other with a footstool for the invisible Lord between them. The psalmist calls upon the Israelites to enter the Lord's dwelling place with him and worship at the Lord's footstool. The Lord swore to set David's offspring on the throne as long as they observed the precepts of the covenant.

Psalm 133 is a psalm of a blessed community. The psalmist describes how good and pleasing it is for a community (Israel) to be gathered as one. It is like the luxury of fine oil running down on the beard of Aaron, the priest, onto the collar of his robe. Oil was used in the consecration of the high priest. It was like the refreshing dew from Hermon, a snow-covered mountain visible from Palestine. The psalmist pictures the dew as watering the mountains of Zion. In Zion, the Lord decreed a blessing of life forever.

Psalm 134, the last of the ascent psalms, calls upon the priests and Levites serving in the Temple during the night to praise the Lord. They are to lift up their hands toward the Lord in prayer to praise the Lord. The psalmist prays for the Lord to bless them from Zion.

Psalm 135 is a song listing the reasons for praising the Lord. Because the Lord chose Jacob as the Lord's treasured possession, the psalmist calls all those in the Temple to praise the goodness of the Lord. Whatever the Lord desires takes place, in heaven, on earth, in the seas, and in the depths.

The Lord caused the death of the firstborn of humans and animals in Egypt, brought wonders against Egypt and Pharaoh, slew the kings of the Amorites, of Bashan, and of Canaan and gave their land to the Israelites. The idols of the nations are merely silver and gold, the work of human hands, with mouths, eyes, ears, and breath that do not work. The psalmist bids the Israelites to bless the Lord, including the priestly houses of Aaron and Levi.

Psalm 136 contains a series of refrains after each line, suggesting the psalm consisted of a singer with a chorus responding. The first three lines praise the Lord who is good, the God of gods, and the Lord of lords. After each of these lines and the following, the chorus responds: "for his mercy endures forever." The remaining lines speak of the Lord performing great wonders, making the heavens, spreading the earth upon the waters, and making the great lights—"the sun to rule the day," and "the moon and stars to rule the night" (136:8, 9).

The psalmist recalls the Exodus experience as reasons for praising the mercy of the Lord. The Lord sent an angel to kill the firstborn of the Egyptians, led the Israelites through the Red Sea, killed the Pharaoh and his army in the Red Sea, and led the people through the desert. The Lord gave the land to the Israelites, freed them from their enemies, and gave them bread. The psalm ends with a call to praise the God of heaven, and once more the refrain "for his mercy endures forever."

Psalm 137 is a psalm of sorrow and hope in exile. The psalmist speaks of the community sitting by the rivers of Babylon. Babylon contained a number of canals. The community, leaving their harps hanging on the poplars in their midst, were unable to sing the songs of Zion in a foreign land. If the psalmist should forget to exalt Jerusalem, then his hand should forget how to work and his tongue stick to the roof of his mouth. He recalls the sin of Edom, a nation that invaded Judah after the Babylonians weakened and destroyed it. Seeking revenge for all Babylon has done to Judah and Jerusalem, the psalmist praises the warriors who would smash the Babylonian children against the rock, which is apparently what the Babylonians did to some of the Israelite children.

Psalm 138 is a psalm of thanksgiving stressing God's protection of the people in every circumstance. The psalmist, bowing toward the Temple, sings songs of thanks to the Lord. He believes when the kings of the earth hear what the Lord has done, they will offer praise and sing of the glory of the Lord. He also believes the Lord will protect him from his enemies, even when he walks amidst dangers.

Psalm 139 exalts God, who knows all, created all, and is present to all. Before the psalmist speaks, the Lord knows what the psalmist is going to say. If the psalmist were to ascend to the heavens, lie down in the grave, fly on the wings of dawn, or dwell beyond the sea, the power of the Lord would know it and protect him. Darkness is not dark enough to hide him. The Lord formed him and knit him in his mother's womb. Even before he was formed, the Lord saw him and listed everything in his life, shaping his life from the beginning. The psalmist professes a fierce hatred for those who hate the Lord and invites the Lord to continue to examine and guide him.

Psalm 140 is an individual lament praying for deliverance from evil. The psalmist begs the Lord to hear his prayer and not allow the plans of the wicked against him to succeed. Never doubting the Lord provides justice for the poor and needy, he prays the wicked will receive a kind of punishment equal to the one they planned for others.

Psalm 141 is an individual lament begging the Lord for protection from evil. The psalmist begs the Lord to set a guard over his mouth, keeping his heart from evil and his actions from wickedness. If he performs evil deeds, he asks the Lord to let a righteous person strike him. He begs the Lord to protect him from the snares of the evil ones, letting them fall into their own traps while he passes over them in safety.

Psalm 142 is an individual lament for help in time of trouble. The psalmist cries out to the Lord for help. His foes have set a trap for him, and, with no human hope for help, he calls out to the Lord, his only refuge on earth. From the depths of his misery, he pleads with the Lord to rescue him from his pursuers who are too strong for him. When the Lord helps him, he knows the righteous will also support him.

Psalm 143 is an individual lament and the last of the seven penitential psalms. The psalmist begs the just Lord to hear his prayer and not to judge him as evil, since no one can be just before the Lord. The enemy has pursued his soul and crushed him, making him dwell in darkness like someone long dead. He reaches out to the Lord like parched land seeking water. He begs the Lord not to hide from him so he will not become like those descending into the dark pit of destruction. For the sake of the name of the Lord, he begs the Lord to lead his soul out of distress and destroy his foes.

Psalm 144 is a royal lament, begging the Lord for victory and prosperity. The king, great as he is, knows he still needs to pray to the Lord for help. The Lord is his safeguard, fortress, deliverer, and shield. In his prayer, he wonders why the Lord takes notice of human beings whose life passes like a fleeting shadow. The king calls upon the Lord to fight on his behalf. In return for the Lord's help, the king promises to sing a new song to the Lord on a ten-stringed instrument. He begs the Lord to deliver him from the sword, just as the Lord delivered David and prays for sons to be like well-attended plants, and daughters as shapely as carved columns in the Temple. In seeking the Lord's blessings, he prays for a full barn, large flocks of sheep, fat oxen, and pleads for safety in the city. The people, who have such safety and whose God is the Lord, are blessed.

Psalm 145 is a psalm about the greatness and goodness of God. The Lord, the true king, is worthy of great praise. All generations praise the goodness of the Lord who is "slow to anger and abounding in mercy" (145:8). The Lord is trustworthy and loving, providing bread for the people and satisfying the desires of all living creatures. The Lord watches over those who are faithful and destroys all the wicked. All human beings praise the Lord forever.

Psalm 146 invites the people to trust in God, the creator. Instead of trusting human beings, the psalmist praises those whose hope is the God of Jacob (Israel), the creator of heaven, the earth, the seas, and all in them. The Lord is faithful forever, providing justice for the oppressed, bread to the hungry, freedom to prisoners, and sight to the blind. The Lord loves the righteous, protects the resident alien, aids the orphans and widows, and frustrates the way of the wicked. The Lord, God of Zion, shall reign forever.

Psalm 147 is a community psalm from the post-exilic era. The psalmist expresses how wonderful it is to praise God who rebuilds Jerusalem and receives the dispersed Israelites back to their homeland. The Lord delights in those who place their trust in the Lord and not in strong horses or the runner's swiftness. The psalmist calls upon Jerusalem and Zion to praise the Lord for strengthening the gates of the city, blessing the children, bringing peace, providing an abundant harvest of wheat, covering the earth with snow and hail, melting them in due season, sending winds, and allowing waters to flow.

Psalm 148 is a call for all of creation to praise the Lord. The psalmist calls on the whole of creation to praise the Lord. The Lord set everything in creation in its place and it will never change. The Lord has given strength to the people, especially to the Israelites who are close to the Lord their God.

Psalm 149 is a song of praise for the Lord, demonstrating the love of Israel for the Lord. The psalmist calls upon the people to sing a new song of praise when they gather in the Temple. The Lord delights in the Israelites and honors the poor with victory. The Israelites bring the Lord's punishment to the nations when they shackle kings and bind nobles in iron chains. The blessings given to Israel offer an example of the glory given to God's faithful.

Psalm 150 is a doxology of praise ending the fifth book of the psalms and the entire Book of Psalms. The psalmist invites the people to praise the Lord in the Temple and in the mighty dome of heaven. In ancient times, people believed a large dome separated the waters above the dome (the sky) from the waters below it (see Genesis 1:6–8). They are to praise the Lord with the horn, harp, lyre, tambourines, strings, pipes, cymbals, and dance. In the final prayer, the psalmist calls every breathing creature to give praise to the Lord. Hallelujah!

Lectio Divina

Spend 8 to 10 minutes in silent contemplation of the following passage:

When the psalmist speaks of offering worship to God in the house of the Lord, he is referring to liturgical, community prayer in the Temple. In Psalm 135, the psalmist writes, "Praise the name of the LORD! Praise, you servants of the LORD, who stand in the house of the LORD, in the courts of the house of our God!" (135:1–2). The psalmist shows us the importance of liturgical worship with the community.

✠ *What can I learn from this passage?*

Review Questions

1. What does Psalm 80 say about the Lord's abandonment of the Israelites?
2. What does Psalm 92 say about a fool's manner of acting?
3. What does Psalm 132 say about the covenant between God and David?

LESSON 5

The Book of Proverbs

Happy the one who finds wisdom, the one who gains understanding! Her profit is better than profit in silver, and better than gold is her revenue (3:13–14).

Opening Prayer (SEE PAGE 15)

Context

Part 1: Proverbs 1—3 The Book of Proverbs offers a series of short, wise sayings meant to guide one's conduct in life. The word "proverb" means "to rule," and the book offers a collection of rules or guides for living well in God's creation. In 1 Kings 5:12–13, the author states Solomon composed 3,000 proverbs, so it was natural that many of the sayings in the Book of Proverbs would be attributed to him, although it is difficult to determine how many proverbs attributed to Solomon were actually from him. Many of the sayings seem to have been written between the late eleventh and early sixth century before Christ.

In Proverbs 1—3, the editor presents the purpose of the book and portrays a father conveying words of wisdom to his son. Wisdom is personified as a woman.

Part 2: Proverbs 4—31 The editor gathers together a collection of proverbs from different sources and contrasts wisdom with foolishness.

PART 1: GROUP STUDY (PROVERBS 1—3)

Read aloud Proverbs 1—3.

1 Introduction and Instruction

Although the opening verse attributes the Book of Proverbs to Solomon, this seems unlikely, as stated in the introduction. Verses 1–7 introduce the purpose of the book, which is to impart wisdom, discipline, and understanding of intelligent sayings. These virtues, in turn, lead to wise conduct and knowing what is just and fair. To the naïve and young, it seeks to convey resourcefulness, knowledge, and prudence; to the wise, advancement in learning and sound guidance to understand a proverb. It contains figures of speech, wise words, and their riddles.

A central theme of the book informs the reader that fear (or reverence) of the Lord is the beginning of knowledge. The foolish despise wisdom and discipline. The editor uses a term, such as "naïve," to refer to all those who are "foolish," as opposed to the "wise."

Verses 8 to 19 contain the warnings of a mother and father to a young man against the enticements of the wicked who invite him to join them in plundering the innocent. These evil people will fall into the trap they set for others and die a cruel death. This is the lot of those bent on evil.

Verses 20 to 31 imagine wisdom as though she were a woman crying out over a city, asking how long the people intend to act as simpletons and reject wisdom. Wisdom calls upon them to listen and receive the spirit of wisdom. Because the people spurned the words of wisdom, wisdom will mock them in a time of terror and not answer when they call. They rejected knowledge, reverence for the Lord, and the counsel of wisdom. As a result, the wicked will be left to their own destruction, while those who obey the words of wisdom will live in security and peace.

2 The Blessings of Wisdom

Using an acrostic of twenty-two verses, which is the number of consonants in the Hebrew alphabet, the parents speak to the young man about the value of wisdom. If he seeks her like silver or a valuable treasure, the Lord will grant him wisdom, reverence for the Lord, and knowledge of God. The Lord will shield the path of the truthful, and prudence and understanding will protect him. He will be saved from the wicked, and from a foreign woman with smooth words who has forsaken her marriage companion and rejects God. She will bring people to the land of the dead from which no one returns. The wise will dwell in peace in the land, while the wicked will be destroyed.

3 Confidence in God Leads to Prosperity

The parents use a series of exhortations consisting of words of wisdom for a just life followed by the reward that will come when one follows these words of wisdom. The young man, who accepts his parent's lessons, who practices love and fidelity, and trusts the Lord rather than his own intelligence, will live many years in peace and find favor with God. In every way, he will live a healthy and vigorous life.

The son who honors the Lord with his wealth and the first fruits of his produce will find his barns and wine vats filled with plenty. If he accepts the rebuke of a disciple of the Lord as though the disciple were a parent, he will receive many blessings. The gifts of wisdom and understanding are more precious than silver, gold, or fine jewels. The wise son will gain a long life, riches, honor, peace, and joy.

The Lord founded the earth by wisdom, established the heavens by understanding, broke open the depths by knowledge, and let the clouds drop down the dew. Wisdom, understanding, and knowledge will bring security, peaceful sleep at night, and the guidance of the Lord. The wise person is careful not to alienate a neighbor by refusing to offer help when able to do so. He does not plot evil against a peaceful neighbor, fight with a neighbor who has done no harm, or envy the violent and choose their ways of acting. To the Lord, the scheming are an abomination, and the just are blessed. The Lord treats sinners as fools and favors with glory the dwelling of the just.

Review Questions

1. What is the purpose of the proverbs of Solomon?
2. What are some words of wisdom the parents share with their son?
3. What rewards does one receive in accepting the words of Lady Wisdom?

Closing Prayer (SEE PAGE 15)

Pray the closing prayer now or after *lectio divina.*

Lectio Divina (SEE PAGE 8)

Relax your body and maintain a posture of prayer (back straight, eyes shut, feet flat on the floor). This exercise can take as long as you want, but in the context of this Bible study, 10 to 20 minutes should be sufficient.

The meditations that follow are provided only to help group participants use this prayer form, but note that *lectio* is intended to bring one to a place of prayerful contemplation where the Word of God speaks to the hearer from his or her heart. (See page 8 for further instruction.)

Introduction and Instruction (1)

Jesus speaks of the message of God being hidden from the wise and the learned and revealed to the childlike (see Luke 10:21). In this case, Jesus is speaking of the wise as those who believe they possess great knowledge, but actually know nothing of creation because they reject the existence of God. The author of the Book of Proverbs says, "Fear of the Lord is the beginning of knowledge" (1:7, see 9:10).

✠ *What can I learn from this passage?*

The Blessings of Wisdom (2)

Those who are wise "will understand what is right and just, what is fair, every good path" (2:9). Living with wisdom guides and protects people from sin. For the author of Proverbs, evil comes from a lack of wisdom and is the domain of fools.

✠ *What can I learn from this passage?*

Confidence in God Leads to Prosperity (3)

Happiness comes from remaining faithful to the Lord and following the Lord's precepts. The wise recognize peace comes from serving the Lord.

✠ *What can I learn from this passage?*

PART 2: INDIVIDUAL STUDY (PROVERBS 4—31)

Day 1: The Wisdom of the Teacher (4—9)

The author is no longer speaking as a father to a son but as a teacher to his disciples, addressing them as "children." He is sharing the wisdom teachings he learned from his father, implying he knows and practices the virtue of wisdom. Wisdom and understanding will protect his children. By practicing and exalting wisdom, they will be exalted.

In verse 10, the author again speaks as a parent to a son. He directs his son not to follow the path of the wicked who eat the bread of wickedness, drink the wine of brutality, and lose sleep if they have not snared anyone. They stumble in darkness, while the just shine like the light at dawn, growing more brilliant as the day progresses. He admonishes his son to remain faithful to his words that bring life and health to those who live by them, and he cautions him to avoid dishonesty in speech, to keep his eyes on the path of wisdom, and never turn toward evil.

Chapter 5 begins with the first of three poems concerning the forbidden woman, which is in contrast to Woman Wisdom. The contrast will be between Woman Wisdom and the foolish woman. The parent warns his son about the stranger (forbidden woman) whose lips drip with the sweetness of honey and her mouth is smoother than oil, but in the end she tastes as bitter as wormwood and is sharp as a two-edged sword. Her path is death, rambling in directions leading to destruction for those who do not keep their eyes on the right path. The teacher urges his son to shun the door of her house, lest he surrender his honor and wealth to the merciless outsider who is the offended husband. The son will rebuke himself for not remaining faithful to the instruction of his parent.

The parent offers advice for the wise to know the blessings of family by remaining faithful to the wife of his youth whose love will excite him. Why should he be intoxicated with another woman? The Lord sees all, knowing that the wicked—who are lost in their own foolishness—will be snared in their own sin and die from a lack of discipline.

In chapter 6, the parent urges his son to free himself from a disturbing pledge he made to a neighbor. He is to forego sleep and flee like a gazelle or a bird from his captives.

The parent uses a comparison with an ant to teach a lesson about wisdom. Just as the ant on its own gathers food in the summer to store provisions for the harvest time, so the son should keep active. If the son slumbers, he will become too lazy to act and find himself besieged by poverty and want. The scoundrels and villains move nervously, plotting evil and discord, but they are suddenly crushed.

The parent declares the Lord hates seven things, namely conceited eyes, a lying tongue, hands that shed innocent blood, a plotting heart, feet hastening to evil, false witnesses, and one who sows dissension in the family.

The son should not reject his father's command or his mother's teaching. He is to remain faithful to their instructions as a lamp guiding him and keeping him from another's wife and the smooth tongue of the foreign woman. A harlot he may gain for a price such as a loaf of bread, but a married woman is a snare for his life. Just as a man cannot take burning embers to his bosom without burning his garments, so the one who sleeps with another's wife will be punished. If someone steals out of need and is caught, that person must still pay sevenfold, but those foolish enough to commit adultery will enrage the husband, who will have the man and woman beaten and disgraced, a reference to a public beating or perhaps to the penalty of death of both parties demanded in Deuteronomy 22:22.

In chapter 7, the father instructs his son to keep his commands and he will live. He advises him to call Wisdom "his sister," and Understanding his "friend." The term sister was used in some ancient cultures to refer to a beloved as "sister," without any reference to kinship. If the son keeps Wisdom as his beloved, he will not be tempted by the foreign woman to commit adultery. The father tells a story about looking from his window and seeing a woman at dusk, dressed like a prostitute, seducing a young man with kisses and telling him about her bed, perfumed and ready for drinking their fill of love until morning, since her husband was away on a journey. The young man follows her, unaware it will cost him his life. The father then speaks to a wider audience addressed as "children," telling them the foreign woman's path leads to death.

Chapter 8 consists of a long speech by Wisdom. She takes up a position where people must pass her, on the top of hills, along the road, at the crossroads and city gates, calling out to all people. She speaks with sincerity and honesty to the intelligent and those who attain knowledge, with instructions and knowledge more valuable than silver and gold, while hating pride, arrogance, and wickedness. She offers counsel, advice, strength, and understanding. Kings, princes, and all judges who have wisdom, govern with justice.

Wisdom claims she loves those who love her, and those who seek her, find her. Riches, honor, long-lasting wealth, and righteousness dwell with her. Her fruit is better than pure gold or silver, filling the treasuries of those who love her.

Wisdom speaks of her preexistence, saying the Lord begot her at the beginning of the Lord's works, the first of the Lord's deeds of long ago. Before the earth was created, she was formed, when there were no seas, no fountains, no springs, no mountains, no earth, no fields, and no chunks of soil. She was there when the Lord established the heavens, the vaults over the sea, the skies above, the springs of the deep, the limits of the sea, and the foundations of the earth and she was the delight of the Lord, playing over the whole earth. She tells the children she rejoices with those who keep her ways, accept her instructions, become wise, and listen at the gates and doorposts. Whoever finds wisdom finds life and is favored by the Lord. Those who ignore or reject wisdom love death.

Chapter 9 begins with Wisdom setting up house and a banquet table. She sends out her maidservants all over the city, inviting the naïve and those who lack sense to come and reject all foolishness in order to live better, advance in understanding, and eat and drink of her wisdom. Those who correct the arrogant or reprove the wicked will earn insults and disgrace. The scoffer who is reproved will hate the one who reproves, but when the wise are rebuked, they will love the one who rebukes. Instruct the wise and they become wiser.

"The beginning of wisdom is fear of the LORD, and knowledge of the Holy One is understanding" (9:10). Wisdom will add days to one's life. The wise are wise for themselves, and the arrogant bear their own burdens.

Woman Folly is boisterous, foolish, and knows nothing. She sits at her door inviting the naïve to come in. She says "Stolen water is sweet," which is apparently an invitation to adultery, meaning stolen sexuality of a married woman is sweet. The naïve do not realize her guests are the dead.

Lectio Divina

Spend 8 to 10 minutes in silent contemplation of the following passage:

Woman Wisdom states she existed before the creation of the world. Although Proverbs appears to be speaking of the wisdom residing in God and not a person, many connect this wisdom to the pre-existence of Jesus, who is the visible image of the wisdom of God in creation. In John's Gospel, we read, "In the beginning was the Word, and the Word was with God, and the Word was God" (John 1:1). The Word and wisdom of God came into the world in the person of Jesus Christ.

✠ *What can I learn from this passage?*

Day 2: First Solomonic Collection of Sayings (10—14)

The proverbs attributed to Solomon consist of a collection of 375 proverbs with no clear arrangements. Almost all the proverbs in chapters 10 to 14 are antithetical, contrasting the wise and the foolish, the just and the wicked, the devout and the pious. The first verse speaks of the people involved in these proverbs, namely the father, the mother, and the son. It tells us: "A wise son gives his father joy, but a foolish son is a grief to his mother." The other proverbs follow.

The just receive God's blessings. They lack nothing, work hard, remain faithful to the Lord, promote peace, nourish the lives of others, live securely and honestly, speak with wisdom, venerate the Lord, and receive a wealth of blessings from the Lord. The life of the wicked and foolish, on the other hand, profits nothing. They live an empty, impoverished life of shame and laziness, rejected by the Lord. They slander, stir up hatred, reject corrections, enjoy wrongdoing, and ignore the Lord. The names of the just will live on in the memory of the people, while the names of the wicked and foolish will be forgotten.

In 1 Peter 4:8, the author writes: "...love covers a multitude of sins," a message taken from Proverbs 10:12 which states: "...love covers all offenses."

Chapter 11 stresses justice, speaking of the just person versus the wicked and faithless one. The just are a delight to the Lord, honest, humble, saved from death, without guile, generous, trustworthy, and merciful. The wicked are an abomination to the Lord, proud, shamed, destined to fail, destructive of others, and merciless. The just keep a confidence, receive protection from the Lord, flourish, obtain blessing to the degree they bless others, and live a long life. The wicked are caught in their own schemes, placing their trust in their empty riches rather than justice and wisdom. The Lord will judge both the just and wicked, and they will receive a judgment in accord with their actions.

Chapter 12 begins by stating the one who loves discipline loves knowledge, while the one who hates to be rebuked is stupid. The just live securely, planning honestly, speaking wisdom, showing kindness, and truthfulness, listening to the counsel and wisdom of others, avoiding useless and slanderous babbling, and living a fulfilling life. The wicked are deceitful, despised, lazy, wise in their own eyes, quick to become angry, always troubled, and an abomination to the Lord.

Chapter 13 begins by contrasting the words of the good with those of the wicked. The mouth of the just brings forth goodness and honesty, while the throat of the wicked produces treachery and violence. The light of the just sows joy, wisdom, and good counsel, while the lamp of the wicked sows discord. The teaching of the wise is like a fountain of life, and those who listen will receive a reward, while those who reject it will face ruin. The just act shrewdly with prudence, but the wicked act foolishly. Those who love their children do not hesitate to discipline them.

Chapter 14 begins by contrasting Wisdom that builds the house with Folly that tears it down. The just revere the Lord and are trustworthy witnesses, whereas those who are devious and lie are lying witnesses. The just offer a guilt offering, finding acceptance before the Lord, but the wicked admit no guilt, leading to their own destruction. Not everything enjoyable is good.

Although the poor and hungry may be despised by their neighbors, the one who is kind to the poor is blessed. Fear of the Lord is a strong refuge and a fountain of life.

Lectio Divina

Spend 8 to 10 minutes in silent contemplation of the following passage:

> Bad news on television dominates to such a degree a person may wonder if evil has conquered the world. The reality is there are many good people in the world, but evil stands out in contrast to the good. Although it may seem like the world is evil, wisdom tells us good people are wiser and receive greater blessings than those who choose the path of evil.

✠ *What can I learn from this passage?*

Day 3: Miscellaneous Proverbs (15—19)

Chapter 15 and the following present a series of proverbs with little relationship to each other, except to offer words of wisdom to the reader. Some of the more significant proverbs are presented in these chapters in this text. The proverbs are based on the fact the Lord sees all, watching the wicked and the good. The sacrifice of the wicked is an abomination to the Lord, but the prayer of the upright is the Lord's delight. Patience and acceptance of very little in life are better than a fortune with anxiety. A wise son prudently seeks counsel from his father. The Lord hears the prayer of the just. A cheerful glance, good news, a helpful rebuke are welcomed by the wise.

Chapter 16 teaches humans make plans, but the Lord produces results which may differ from the plans. For a successful outcome, human beings should entrust their plans to the Lord. The wise are esteemed for discernment, good sense, and words of wisdom, while the foolish choose silliness. "Gray hair is a crown of glory," gained by a just life. It is better to be patient and in control of one's temper than to choose to battle.

Chapter 17 states a crust with quiet is better than a feast filled with strife. Those who mock the poor or rejoice over their plight revile their Maker. Grandchildren are the glory of the elderly. Overlooking an offense promotes friendship; gossip separates friends. Those who rebel will encounter rebellion. Evil will not leave one who returns evil for good. A quarrel opens a dam, so avoid a quarrel.

A friend is like a brother who helps in time of adversity. The joyful have good health; the depressed spirit dries up the bones. A guilty person accepts a bribe and distorts justice. A discerning person is wise; a fool looks only for earthly gain. A foolish son brings aggravation and sorrow to his parents. Those who are discreet and watch their words are intelligent. Even fools look intelligent if they keep silent.

Chapter 18 states the alienated seek a pretext for beginning a quarrel. Fools do not seek understanding, but only their own opinion. The just find refuge in the Lord. The haughty heart leads to disaster; the humble heart to honor. Those who answer before listening are foolish. A good spirit supports one who is ill; a broken spirit does not. The tongue brings death or life to the person who chooses to use it well or not. Finding a wife is finding happiness, a favor given by the Lord. Some friends are not helpful and bring ruin, but true friends are more loyal than brothers.

In chapter 19, the author says it is better to be impoverished than be rich and crooked. Although many are willing to lie for the sake of the law, the false witness will not escape punishment. Being slow to anger and overlooking an offense is wisdom. The foolish son can ruin his father and a quarrelsome wife is like constantly dripping water, wearing down the spirit. Those who follow the commands of the Lord live, and those who despise the commands will die. Whoever cares for the poor will receive a full payment back from the Lord. Fear of the Lord leads to life, allowing a person to eat and sleep with security. "Whoever mistreats a father or drives away a mother, is a shameless and disgraceful child."

Lectio Divina

Spend 8 to 10 minutes in silent contemplation of the following passage:

When the disciples of John the Baptist asked Jesus if he was the Messiah, he told them the blind see, the lame walk, lepers are cleansed, the deaf hear, and the dead are raised. The miracles of Jesus prove he is the Christ. At the end of this list, he adds what seems most important to him, saying, "...and the poor have the good news proclaimed to them" (Matthew 11:5). The Book of Proverbs often equates helping those who are poor with wisdom.

✠ *What can I learn from this passage?*

Day 4: The Sayings of the Wise (20—24)

Chapter 20 says an honorable person avoids strife, while a fool starts quarrels. The just who walk in integrity bring happiness to their children. Those who claim they are free of sin may be deceiving themselves. Honesty is more valuable than gold and abundant jewels. Those who curse mother or father will have the light go out of their life. Wait for the Lord to repay evil. The pride of youth is strength; the splendor of the aged is gray hair.

Chapter 21 claims that, in the eyes of the one acting, all deeds are correct, but the Lord sees the heart. A proud and arrogant heart is sinful. The path may be confusing and wandering, but one's conduct should remain blameless and right. Those who ignore the poor will be ignored when they cry out. Justice and kindness will lead to a good life and honor. A wise person can overwhelm the strong. Those who speak carefully keep themselves from trouble. The sluggards will slay themselves with laziness. A sacrifice from the wicked is an abomination, more so when offered with a bad motive. No wisdom, understanding, or counsel will prevail over the Lord.

In chapter 22, wisdom teaches that a good name is more desirable than great wealth. The generous will be blessed for sharing their food with the poor. Getting rid of the arrogant also means getting rid of conflict and abuse. It is useless to oppress the poor or give to the rich to enrich oneself.

The Words of the Wise, a collection of wise sayings from 22:17 to 24:22, begins as the author calls the reader to listen to his teachings or to hold onto them if they are already speaking about them. He seems to be writing for youth choosing a career. Portions of this advice come from an ancient Egyptian composition written around 1100 BC. The Egyptian manuscript contained thirty chapters.

The author warns the youth not to rob the poor or crush the needy at the gate, which was the place where accusations against others were made and judged. The Lord is on the side of the poor and needy, ready to defend them and to plunder those who plunder them. According to ancient law, a landmark established a person's land boundaries, and moving a landmark is akin to stealing land.

In chapter 23, the lessons continue. When the young people sit down to dine with a king, the teacher counsels them about table etiquette, telling them to stick the knife in their gullet, which means they should not eat like a glutton. Since seizing the delicacies would identify the youth as foolish gluttons, the teacher advises them to avoid the delicacies. Even if a person were invited to dine with a king, it would be improper for a guest to eat before a ruler eats unless invited to do so.

Youth should not dine with miserly hosts. Even if they tell the youth to eat and drink, such people are doing it for convention's sake and do not mean it.

The redeemer of the fatherless family is usually a male relative who protects the family. The author warns the youth the redeemer is strong and will defend the cause of the family.

The teacher turns his attention to matters concerning the development of youths. He instructs youths to apply themselves to instruction and learn wisdom. They are not to envy sinners but must venerate the Lord. Since drunkards and gluttons live in poverty and their drowsing leads them to wear rags for clothing, the youth are neither to join with wine drinkers nor with those who load themselves with meat. A person's mother and father will rejoice when they see the wisdom of their child.

The teacher vividly describes the effects of too much drink. He speaks of the drunkard screaming, shouting with bleary eyes, and spending too much time over wine. He warns the youth to avoid the red, sparkling wine that goes down smoothly but in the end is poison for them. Their eyes begin to see strange sights; they experience incoherent thoughts; they are like one sleeping on the rolling waves of the high seas; they feel no pain, and they ask when they can go out and get wine.

In chapter 24, the teacher warns youths not to envy the wicked or to join them in plotting violence. The wise and learned are more powerful than the strong. The teacher says being unaware of the needs of a neighbor is no excuse.

The Lord, the searcher of hearts, knows all and will repay them according to their deeds. Wisdom is as sweet for the soul as honey is sweet to the taste.

Chapter 24:23–34 belongs to a segment of the Book of Proverbs that begins with the statement: "There also are Words of the Wise." The teacher warns against showing partiality by freeing a guilty person. The one who acts this way will be cursed by the nations, while the one who renders a just judgment will fare well and become prosperous.

The teacher declares an honest reply and a kiss on the lips are signs of affection and respect. The teacher warns against testifying against a neighbor, thus being insincere in kissing a neighbor, which was meant to be a gesture of honesty. The sluggard welcomes a little sleep that actually becomes a long sleep, and, as a result, he experiences poverty and want, which come upon him like a robber.

Lectio Divina

Spend 8 to 10 minutes in silent contemplation of the following passage:

The teacher of Wisdom speaks of "an honest reply—a kiss." To the Israelites, a kiss was a form of greeting signifying affection and honesty. The statement in Proverbs calls to mind Judas, who chose to identify Jesus to the crowd with a kiss (see Luke 22:47–48). Judas showed extreme dishonesty by using a gesture of affection and honesty in betraying Jesus. Some people feign sincere concern for others while secretly plotting to hurt them.

✠ *What can I learn from this passage?*

_____

Day 5: Second Solomonic Collection (25—31)

Although many of the proverbs attributed to Solomon were not written by him, the fifth part of the Book of Proverbs begins with: "These also are proverbs of Solomon. The servants of Hezekiah, king of Judah, transmitted them." Although there was a king of Judah from 715 to 687 BC named Hezekiah, the "servants of Hezekiah" appears to refer to scribes, not the king. The word "also" in the opening line (25:1) points to an earlier collection of proverbs, most likely those found earlier in the Book of Proverbs (10—22:16).

The proverbs tell us that kings should be able to understand the Lord more fully than others, while others are not able to know the heart of a king. People should not claim a place of honor in the presence of a king, aware it is better to be invited to come up closer than to be humiliated before the prince.

The youths are to speak privately with their opponent and not reveal what they know about others, lest these others hear about it and cause shame for the offender.

Those who boast of giving a gift without actually giving it are like clouds and wind with no rain. Just as people should not eat more sweet honey than they need, lest they vomit it up, so one should visit a neighbor on seldom occasions, lest they have their fill of them and hate them. Those who bear false witness against a neighbor are like the force of a club, sword, or sharp arrow. Those who give food and drink to their enemies will heap burning coals on their heads.

Chapter 26 begins by saying honor for a fool is as out of place as snow in summer or rain at harvest time. Fools should be answered in accord with their foolishness to keep them from becoming wise in their own estimation. Just as dogs return to their vomit, so fools repeat their foolishness. There is more hope for fools than those who are wise in their own estimation.
The sluggard claims there is a lion in the street to avoid going out. The sluggard foolishly believes he is wiser than seven people with good judgment.

The words of the talebearer sink into the heart of another like dainty morsels. The words of the deceitful person, who pretends concern, cannot be trusted. The words of a liar are his own enemy, making him fall into a deep pit.

Chapter 27 states people should not praise themselves but allow another to praise them. A fool's frustration is heavier than stone or sand. Anger is bad enough, but jealousy is worse. A friend's blows are more trustworthy than the kisses of an enemy. For the hungry person, even bitter food tastes sweet. Trust a friend rather than family in time of trouble. A close neighbor is better than a relative far away. The wise hide from evil, while the foolish relish it and pay the penalty.

A quarrelsome wife is like "a persistent leak on a rainy day" and as unable to be restrained as "a stormwind" (27:15–16). Wealth does not last forever, nor does a king. When new growth appears, lambs provide clothing, and goats will provide milk and food.

In chapter 28, the author states the wicked live in fear and the good live in peace. The wise son heeds instruction, while a son who joins with evil disgraces his father. The one who becomes wealthy by charging interest (which was forbidden to the Jews of ancient times) will eventually lose it to those who help the poor. Those who lead the just into wickedness will fall into their own pit, while the just will attain prosperity. "The rich are wise in their own eyes, but the poor who are intelligent see through them" (28:11).

When the just triumph, people rejoice, but when the wicked triumph, people hide. Those who do not admit their sins do not prosper, while those who confess them and repent receive mercy. The trustworthy will be blessed; the one seeking illicit wealth will be punished. Partiality, even in a small matter, is wrong. Misers find want instead of riches. The greedy stir up strife; the faithful prosper. Those trusting in themselves are fools; the wise are safe. Those who give to the poor lack nothing; those who look the other way are cursed.

Chapter 29 says people rejoice when the just flourish but groan when the wicked rule. Whoever loves wisdom brings joy to his father; he who consorts with harlots squanders his wealth. Scoffers enflame people; the wise calm them. Disputing with a fool leads to railing and ridicule but no resolution. Fools give vent to their anger; the wise control it. The rod of correction results in wisdom; youths who remain uncontrolled give disgrace to their mothers. Discipline the children and they will be a blessing. The one who follows instruction is blessed. Haughtiness brings humiliation; humility acquires honor. The evildoer is an abomination to the just; the just an abomination to the wicked.

Chapter 30 claims to be the words of an unknown person named Agur, who is from Massa in northern Arabia. He begins by speaking about being a weary human who is less human because he lacks wisdom and does not know the holy one. He asks who has ascended to the heavens and returned, captured the wind in his hand, bound the waters in a cloak, and established the ends of the earth. The answer, of course, is no one. The Lord is a shield for those who need protection.

The author writes about four kinds of sinners, namely those who curse their parents, those who remain in their sins although they believe they are sinless, those who are overbearing and proud, and those who devour those in need and the poor. Like leeches who suck blood, they never have enough. Four things are never satisfied, namely death, the barren womb, the parched land thirsty for water, and fire for fuel.

The author speaks of four things he cannot understand, namely the gliding of an eagle, the slithering of a snake without feet, the movement of a ship on the high seas, and the way of a man with a woman. The adulterous woman easily discounts her wrongdoing after partaking of its pleasures.

There are four things that are confusing, namely a slave who becomes a king, an undeserving fool glutted with food, an unloved woman who finds a husband, and a maid who replaces her mistress. Four things are so small yet so wise, namely the ant that stores up food in the summer, the badgers that hide among the crags, the locusts that march in formation with no leader, and lizards that find their way into the king's palace. Four things are stately, namely the lion that never backs down before anything, the strutting rooster, the he-goat, and the king leading the people.

Chapter 31 claims to be the instruction of the mother of Lemuel, the king of Massa. The queen mother counsels her son not to give himself to women who ruin kings. She warns him against drinking wine that would lead him to ignore his duty and mistreat those who are in need. He can give the wine to those who are dying or to bitter people. Drink will enable them to forget their misery and troubles. The king should speak on behalf of the mute, judging justly in defending the needy and poor.

A woman of worth is more valuable than jewels and difficult to find. The author praises the worthy wife. Her husband trusts her judgment. She brings him gain all her days. Like a merchant ship, she secures provisions from afar. While it is still night, she rises to distribute portions of food to her household and maidservants. She acquires a field and plants a vineyard. Her character is strong and forceful, gaining profit from her undertaking and working late. She generously reaches out to the needy.

When it snows, her household is doubly clothed. She brings pride to her husband, who sits in prominence at the city gates with the elders. She can laugh at the future, and she speaks with wisdom. She oversees the affairs of the household and does not eat the bread of others (idleness). Her husband

and children praise her, telling her she exceeds all women of proven worth. Charm and beauty are fleeting, but the true measure of a woman of worth is her reverence for the Lord.

Lectio Divina

Spend 8 to 10 minutes in silent contemplation of the following passage:

The author of Proverbs writes: "If your enemies are hungry, give them food to eat, if thirsty, give something to drink; For live coals you will heap on their heads, and the Lord will vindicate you" (25:21–22). Paul quotes this proverb in his Letter to the Romans (12:20) when he urges the people to avoid becoming like the offender in seeking revenge. He is saying goodness will surprise and even hurt the offender more than revenge.

✠ *What can I learn from this passage?*

Review Questions

1. What image of Woman Wisdom does the author of chapter 8 give?
2. What does Wisdom say about concern for the poor?
3. What are some virtues of the woman of worth in chapter 31?

The Books of Ecclesiastes and the Song of Songs

There is an appointed time for everything, and a time for every affair under the heavens (Ecclesiastes 3:1).

Opening Prayer (SEE PAGE 15)

Context

Part 1: Ecclesiastes 1—3 The Book of Ecclesiastes is a cynical book, stressing the vanity of life. It was apparently written around the third century before Christ, at a time when Judea was dominated by the Hellenistic kings from Egypt who were ruthless in exploiting the powerless people of Judea. The author of Ecclesiastes, named Qoheleth, is identified as David's son, which could mean he belongs to the line of David, rather than referring to an immediate son of David. Since Qoheleth is aware of the oppression and feels the futility of life, he is not completely joyless. He instructs the people to enjoy what they have.

In the first three chapters, the author describes all in life as "vanity of vanities" since there is an appointed time for everything under the sun, and no one will escape his or her appointed time for birth, for life, and for death. The best thing to do is to eat, drink, and provide for their needs, because all will end in the grave.

Part 2: Ecclesiastes 4—12; Song of Songs 1—8 In Ecclesiastes, Qoheleth challenges those who believe the bad live a shorter life than the good or the wicked live with greater misery than the good. In the end, a person should fear God and keep the Lord's commands because the Lord will judge all the works performed on earth, whether good or bad.

The Song of Songs is a love song extolling the gift of human sexuality and the sacredness of marriage.

PART 1: GROUP STUDY (ECCLESIASTES 1—3)

Read aloud Ecclesiastes 1—3.

1—2 Vanity of Vanities

The superscript identifies the words of Ecclesiastes as coming from "Qoheleth," a king in Jerusalem. The author speaks as a son of David. Since Solomon was a gatherer of wisdom, the image of a king who is a son of David evokes images of Solomon. The Hebrew word, Qoheleth, means an assembler or gatherer. The book begins with the phrase: "Vanity of vanities! All things are vanity." The word vanity refers to a breath or vapor, meant to show that the life of human beings passes away like a vapor. People toil under the sun and one generation gives way to the next. The author says "under the sun" a number of times rather than using the term "under the heavens." He is speaking of the living, not those in the darkness of the grave.

Qoheleth speaks of the daily occurrences of life, saying the sun rises and sets in the same place, the wind blows from various directions, all rivers flow to the sea without filling it up, the eye does not see enough, and the ear does not hear enough. "Nothing is new under the sun!" (1:9) Even when something appears to be new it already existed in previous ages.

After searching, he concludes all on earth is like wind. The crooked cannot be made straight and no one can count what is not there. He decides great wisdom leads to great sorrow.

Chapter 2 speaks of an abundance which reflects that of Solomon (see 1 Kings 4–11). Qoheleth tried pleasure, laughter, wine, building grand houses, planting vineyards, gardens, parks, and fruit trees. He acquired male and female slaves, owned vast herds of cattle and flocks of sheep. Accumulating every sort of treasure, he soon realized in his wisdom that all was vanity and a chase after the wind. Even a king who succeeds a king can only do what was done before.

The king realized wise people can see what fools who walk in darkness cannot see, but in the end both die. Since, for him, all work is bad, he hated life, realizing it is simply vanity, a chase after wind.

The king will be leaving the fruits of his toil to the one who is to come after him, whether a wise or foolish person. Despite all his wisdom, knowledge, and skill, his legacy will go to one who did not work for it. What profit do human beings receive from all their work and anxiousness? Day and night, sorrow and grief are the occupation of humans.

Despite his skepticism, the king does not reject life completely. He advocates eating, drinking, and providing good things from one's work. This is a gift from God. God gives wisdom, knowledge, and joy to the good, while those who displease God work and gather possessions that will be given to the one who pleases God. This is also vanity.

3 An Appointed Time for Everything

Using fourteen pairs of opposites in a rhythmic fashion, the author speaks of the times already appointed by God. The first eight verses state in ho-hum and skeptical fashion fourteen pairs of opposites, with two opposites in each verse. There is a time to give birth, a time to die, a time to plant, a time to uproot, — a time to kill, a time to heal, a time to tear down, a time to build, — a time to weep, a time to laugh, a time to mourn, a time to dance, — a time to scatter stones, a time to gather them, a time to embrace, a time to keep far from embraces, — a time to seek, a time to lose, a time to keep, a time to cast away, — a time to rend, a time to sew, a time to be silent, a time to speak, — a time to love, a time to hate, a time of war, and a time of peace.

The author asks what gain workers receive from their toil, expecting no answer to his question. Human beings have received a sense of past and future, but they cannot fathom what God has done from beginning to end. There is nothing better human beings can do except to be happy and do well during their life. God gives human beings the gift of eating, drinking, and taking pleasure in their toil. What God does lasts forever, with nothing added to it or taken from it. God has done this so people may be in awe of God.

Wickedness exists in the world, even in places where one would expect justice. Humans and animals will both go down into dust. Who can determine if the life breath of humans ascends upward and the life breath of animals goes downward to the earth. Because this is the lot of human beings, Qoheleth affirms human beings have nothing better to do than to take pleasure in their toil.

Review Questions

1. What does Qoheleth mean when he speaks of the "vanity of vanities?"
2. What conclusion does Qoheleth reach when he studies the life of those who seek profit in life?
3. What does Qoheleth mean when he says there is an appointed time for everything under the sun?

Closing Prayer (SEE PAGE 15)

Pray the closing prayer now or after *lectio divina*.

Lectio Divina (SEE PAGE 8)

Relax your body and maintain a posture of prayer (back straight, eyes shut, feet flat on the floor). This exercise can take as long as you want, but in the context of this Bible study, 10 to 20 minutes should be sufficient.

The meditations that follow are provided only to help group participants use this prayer form, but note that *lectio* is intended to bring one to a place of prayerful contemplation where the Word of God speaks to the hearer from his or her heart. (See page 8 for further instruction.)

Vanity of Vanities (1—2)

Ecclesiastes seems to drain hope out of living, saying all toil is like a puff of wind and human beings might as well enjoy what they have. It presents a bleak picture of the destiny of human beings who have no hope for resurrection. Once they die, all is ended—vanity of vanities. Paul the Apostle bases belief in our resurrection on the resurrection of Jesus Christ. He writes, "For if the dead are not raised, neither has Christ been raised" (1 Corinthians 15:16). Resurrection of the dead leads to hope.

✠ *What can I learn from this passage?*

An Appointed Time for Everything (3)

In Ecclesiastes, the author cynically tells us there is nothing new under the sun. Unlike the author of Ecclesiastes, most of us view the time for birth and death, for planting and uprooting, for weeping and laughing as part of the human condition that points to a wise God of creation who is always ready to help us. We believe each day brings new opportunities for marvelous developments in life. Life is not drudgery but a challenge.

✠ *What can I learn from this passage?*

PART 2: INDIVIDUAL STUDY (ECCLESIASTES 4—12; SONG OF SONGS 1—8)

Day 1: Gain and Loss (Ecclesiastes 4—6:9)

Qoheleth offers a series of maxims illustrating the vanity of life. He declares those who are dead are better off than the living and those unborn better yet, because they have not witnessed the evil taking place under the sun. He witnesses the vanity of a solitary person with no family, who works endlessly and finds no satisfaction in wealth. "Two are better than one" because they receive a good wage for their toil, help each other if one falls, keep each other warm by sleeping together, and are able to resist others like a three-ply cord which is not easily broken.

One can come from prison and become king to lead many, but those who are later led by another king after him forget him. This is vanity and chasing after the wind.

In chapter 5, Qoheleth warns against making hasty promises to God. When people make a vow to the Lord, they should fulfill it as soon as possible. It is better not to make a vow than to make a vow and not fulfill it. In all situations, good and bad, a person should remain in awe of God.

When the people see an arrogant person oppressing the poor, they should not be surprised, since the arrogant high official has someone higher watching him, and above that person is still a higher person.

Those who covet riches are never satisfied. The laborer can sleep peacefully; the wealth of the rich keeps them from peaceful sleep. Riches hoarded by owners often leads to their harm. If they lose their wealth through some adversity, they have nothing to provide for their children. They came from their mother's womb naked and they will return naked. All their days are spent in fear of death.

In chapter 6, Qoheleth declares he has seen situations where one with wealth, property, honor, a hundred children, and a long life was not able to enjoy them. A child born dead and left unburied is better off than such a person. In the end, no matter how long the worried rich person lives, that person and the dead child go to the same place.

"All human toil is for the mouth" (human desire), which is never satisfied. What profit do the wise have over fools, or what profit do the lowly have in conducting themselves in this life? The answer is the profit for both types is enjoying what they see or possess rather than what they desire without possessing.

Lectio Divina

Spend 8 to 10 minutes in silent contemplation of the following passage:

In Paul's era, many people had the same idea about death expressed in Ecclesiastes and had to be taught the dead as well as the living will share in resurrection to a new life in Christ (see 1 Thessalonians 4:13–17). Paul had to teach them death was not the end of everything.

✠ *What can I learn from this passage?*

Day 2: Qoheleth's Conclusions (Ecclesiastes 6:10—8:17)

Mortals cannot contend with one who is stronger, namely God. Who really knows what is good for mortals whose vain life passes like a shadow? Who can tell them what comes afterward?

Qoheleth lists a series of "better...than" statements found in Proverbs, with the intent of challenging many sayings accepted as wise. He lists good and bad proverbs. A good name is better than ointment; the day of death than the day of birth; mourning than feasting; sorrow than laughter; the acceptance of rebuke than the song of fools; the end of a thing than its beginning; and a patient spirit than a proud one. Wisdom is good to possess and profitable for those who live, seeing the sun. Wisdom should be protected like money, and knowledge is profitable because wisdom bestows life for those who possess it. Consider creation and ask how one can make straight what God made crooked.

Wisdom, in the end, is enjoying good things on good days, and reflecting on evil days. In order for no one to find fault with God, God made both. Qoheleth has seen the just perishing and the wicked living long lives. His advice is a person should not be overly just or wicked. What is important for success is to act with fear of the Lord. Real wisdom states there is no one on earth who does not sin. The wise weigh what they hear, not accepting everything as truth.

Qoheleth sought wisdom, but it eluded him in the same way it eludes everyone else. He speaks of finding Folly, which he pictures as a woman setting a trap for him. The one who pleases God will escape her trap, but the one who displeases God will be captured. God made human beings honest, but they sought other ways of acting.

In chapter 8, Qoheleth exalts the wise person who can explain many things. The sage must follow the command of the king without asking the king what he is doing. The wise obey the king's command. No matter how much wisdom a person has, it is still limited because he is ignorant about what the judgment will bring and the day of death.

Qoheleth appears to be confused when he first writes wicked people are evil because they seem to be rewarded since the sentence they deserve is not immediately imposed on them. The wicked sin over and over and survive. Those who act justly are forgotten. Qoheleth then corrects the statement by saying he knows all will go well with the person who reveres the Lord, and all will not go well with the wicked. This correction may be added by a later writer who wanted to protect the idea of the good being rewarded and the evil being punished.

Qoheleth sees vanity in the good and evil deeds on earth. Some of the just are treated as having done evil, and some of those who do evil are treated as though they have acted justly. Because there is nothing better for human beings under the sun than to eat, drink, and be joyful, he praises joy during their limited period of toil on earth. His conclusion is no one can claim to know God's work under the sun.

Lectio Divina

Spend 8 to 10 minutes in silent contemplation of the following passage:

Some proverbs speak of the early death and suffering of the wicked, but Qoheleth says many of the wicked prosper. Without a belief in life after death, it was difficult to understand what punishment the wicked endured. With belief in life after death, Paul the Apostle writes, "Make no mistake: God is not mocked, for a person will reap only what he sows" (Galatians 6:7).

✠ *What can I learn from this passage?*

Day 3: No One Knows the Future (Ecclesiastes 9—12)

Qoheleth struggles with trying to understand God's plan. Whether one is wicked or good, spiritually clean or unclean, faithful in offering sacrifices to God or not, or reckless in taking an oath or not, all die. Those who are living know they will die, but the dead no longer have any knowledge of anything under the sun. As a result, the living should enjoy their bread and wine, wear fine garments, and perfume their heads while they perform their work under the sun. Like fish in a net or birds in a snare, human beings are caught by death.

Qoheleth tells of a king surrounding a small city with few inhabitants. In the city lives a wise person who could save the city, but because of his lowly position, no one listens to him. The people would rather listen to the foolish words of a ruler. Wisdom is more powerful than war, but one fool can deter people from attending to wisdom.

In chapters 10 to 12:8, Qoheleth lists a series of short proverbs. Just as a fly corrupts oil, a little folly corrupts wisdom. Remain calm, even if confronted with the anger of a ruler. Fools often rule while the great and rich remain in a lower place. People's actions may destroy them. For instance, a man digging a pit may fall into it; a man breaking through a wall may be bitten by a snake; a man quarrying stone may be hurt by the stone; and a man chopping wood may be hurt by the wood. A dull ax leads to greater exertion, while wisdom leads to success. Skills depend on their proper and prompt use. A charmer bitten before charming is useless. Words from the wise win favor, while the multitude of words of a fool consume them, moving from foolishness to madness. No one knows the future.

A land ruled by a young king or princes partying all night is to be pitied, while the land ruled by a king of noble birth and princes who eat and drink at the proper time is blessed. Laziness leads to a sagging or leaking house. A feast leads to laughter; wine to joy, and money to fulfillment of every need. Words uttered in private may fly to others as though carried on the wings of a bird.

Chapter 11 begins with proverbs concerning trading on the waters. Those who trade their wealth on the waters and who risk "seven, or even eight portions" may find great profit. Seven or eight portions is a way of saying the one who risks more can gain more. Humans cannot control a full cloud which brings rain. The one who pays too much attention to the wind which one cannot control will never sow the seed, and the one who worries about the clouds bringing rain will never reap. Just as a person does not know how life's breath enters a person in the womb, so people do not know the work of God.

A person who sows in the morning should not be idle at night, thereby sowing only when it is the perfect time for it and losing other opportunities for a more abundant harvest.

While enjoying the light of the sun, a person should remember death will bring many days of darkness. All is vanity. Qoheleth tells the young to rejoice in youth and follow their heart, reminding themselves God will judge them. They should avoid misery and pain, knowing "youth and black hair are fleeting."

Many commentators view chapter 12 as an allegory concerning aging, while others view it as an eschatological image of the decay of creation. Qoheleth urges youth to remember their Creator before evil days of old age capture them. For those who view Qoheleth's imagery in this chapter as an allegory concerning human beings, the images used would then express the aging of the human body—the weakening of the guardians of the house (the arms), the strong men (the legs), the women who grind (the teeth), those who look (the eyes), the doors (the lips), the daughters of songs (the voice), the almond tree blooms (the white hair), the sluggish movement of the locust (the stiffness of old age), and the caper berry (a stimulant for one's failing appetite). The youth are to remember all this before they die. Qoheleth uses the image of a golden bowl as an image of life. With the snapping of a silver cord holding it, it breaks. He then uses the image of a broken pulley at a well allowing a pitcher to shatter. All dust (humans) return to earth, and life breath returns to God. This is a reference to Genesis 2:7 where God forms Adam out of the dust of the earth and breathes life into him.

Qoheleth uses the same expression at the end as he used at the beginning: "Vanity of vanities, says Qoheleth, all things are vanity" (1:2; 12:8).

In an epilogue, a later writer notes Qoheleth was a wise man who taught, examined, and arranged proverbs, carefully writing down true sayings with exactness. These are firmly established sayings of one shepherd. The writer warns readers not to search for more proverbs which are extensive and which could weary the reader.

In summary, the author calls upon readers to show reverential awe before God, keeping the Lord's commandments, which apply to all people. God will judge all human endeavors, hidden as well as seen, good as well as bad.

Lectio Divina

Spend 8 to 10 minutes in silent contemplation of the following passage:

Paul the Apostle confronts those who would follow the advice of Ecclesiastes. He notes: "If the dead are not raised: Let us eat and drink, for tomorrow we die" (1 Corinthians 15:32), which he views as a sinful way of thinking.

✠ *What can I learn from this passage?*

Day 4: The Words of Lovers (Song of Songs 1—5:1)

The use of the title "Song of Songs" at the beginning of the book is meant to connote a superlative, meaning this is the greatest of songs. Although the book refers to Solomon, this is unlikely since the book was written at a date long after the death of Solomon, after the Babylonian captivity ended in 538 BC. In the *New American Bible*, revised edition, the translation of each section begins with a *W, M,* or *D* to aid the reader in determining whether it is a woman (*W*), a man (*M*), or the Daughters of Jerusalem (*D*) speaking. The book portrays the splendor of human sexuality found in marriage. It contains expressions of love, sensuality, longing, and courtship.

The woman speaks of allowing her lover to kiss her with the "kisses of his mouth," declaring his love is better than wine. There is a play on words in the original Hebrew text linking kisses with wine. In ancient texts, drinking wine was frequently used to refer to lovemaking. In the Book of Proverbs, the author uses a similar image when he writes: "Come, let us drink our fill of love, until morning, let us feast on love" (Proverbs 7:18). In the Hebrew, the word for "perfume" and "name" is similar, allowing the author to use a play on words and say the man's name is flowing perfume, which lures women to love him.

The woman refers to the man as a king who brought her into his bed chambers. The term "king" could refer to a king or to someone she admires as though a king. The woman invites her female companions to join her in praising her lover.

Speaking in the first person, the woman addresses the "Daughters of Jerusalem," saying she is black and beautiful, an apparent reference to the dark tents of Qedar in the Syrian desert and the curtains of Solomon, which could also be read as the curtains of Salma, a region close to Qedar. She claims she is blackened by the sun because she had to care for her brothers' vineyards, and not her own. Her vineyard could be a reference to herself. She addresses her lover as a shepherd, which is a common reference applied to a king in the Old Testament, and she asks where he shepherds his flocks and where he rests at midday, possibly a veiled reference to a time when they could engage in lovemaking.

The man begins to speak in verse 8. He tells the woman to follow the tracks of the flock, alluding to her also as a shepherd pasturing her sheep. In verse 9, he compares her adornment as equal to the adornment of a royal chariot of Pharaoh and speaks of the beauty of her cheeks and neck.

In verse 12, the woman speaks about her perfumes (spikenard was a perfumed ointment) and the sweet smells of her lover (myrrh and a cluster of henna) as he lies between her breasts. She praises his beauty and describes the verdant couch and firmness of their house.

In chapter 2, her lover describes her as a lily among thorns (women). She speaks of her lover as a fragrant, luring apple tree among trees (men). She sits in the shadow of his protection, enjoying his fruit. She states he brings her to this banquet hall where his glance signals lovemaking. He holds and embraces her. She orders the Daughters of Jerusalem not to stir up love until the time is right, an apparent caution to the Daughters of Jerusalem not to awaken her lover.

She pictures her lover leaping over the mountains and hills like a gazelle or a young stag. He peeks through the windows and lattices. Since it is springtime, he invites her to come with him, addressing her as a dove that hides in the crevices of the cliff, out of sight of others. The woman notes foxes (men) are in the vineyards, which are in bloom. The vineyards in bloom are a reference to women in their sexual blossoming sought after by young men. The woman uses a marriage reference by saying her lover belongs to her and she to him. She states her lover feeds among the lilies, a reference to the delights the lover finds in her.

In chapter 3, the woman lying in her bed at night longs for her beloved and rises to search for him in the city. When she finds him, she holds him and does not let him go. She takes him to the chamber of her mother's house. The events show the anxious desire of a woman in love seeking her beloved and the acceptance of their relationship by her mother.

In an apparent addition to the poem in 3:6, the Daughters of Jerusalem ask who is coming up from the desert like a column of smoke, and identifies the man as Solomon, her lover, in the company of sixty valiant men of Israel carrying their swords to protect "against the terrors of the night" (bandits). King Solomon, carried on an elaborate throne with columns of silver, a roof of gold, and a seat of purple cloth, appears to be arriving in a wedding procession. The Daughters of Jerusalem go out to see the king, who was crowned by his mother on the joyful day of his marriage.

In chapter 4, the man speaks of the beauty of the woman, with eyes like doves, hair like a prosperous flock of goats coming down Mount Gilead, teeth as white as a flock of sheep, lips like scarlet, a mouth so beautiful, cheeks as red as pomegranate halves, neck like a tower of David, and breasts like two fawns. Until the day becomes cool, the man shall enjoy the breasts which are like the mountain of fragrant myrrh and the hill of sweet smelling frankincense. He does not wish to be separated from her by mountains or the lair of beasts.

The man declares his lover has ravished his heart with one glance. He addresses her as "sister," a term often used in ancient times as a term of endearment rather than a term of physical relationship. He praises his bride, declaring her love is better than wine and her fragrance richer than any expensive spice. Her lips are like honey and her fragrance like the fragrance of the forests of Lebanon.

The lover views his beloved as a lush, enclosed garden, filled with every form of sweet perfume and refreshing streams. He calls upon the winds to spread this perfume everywhere. The woman takes the last line of verse 16, inviting her lover to come and eat of the choicest fruit of the garden.

In chapter 5, verse 1, the man has come to his bride ("my garden"), prepared to enjoy all the sweetness and pleasure possible which is symbolized by myrrh, honeycomb and honey, wine and milk. Lovers drink deeply with satisfaction, symbolized by food and drink.

Lectio Divina

Spend 8 to 10 minutes in silent contemplation of the following passage:

> According to the Song of Songs, sensual desire is a blessing bestowed by God on a man and woman who are married to each other. Jewish and Christian scholars view the Song of Songs as pointing beyond itself to the intense intimacy existing between God and human beings, an intimacy as close as the intimacy of marriage where, in God's plan, the two become one.

✠ *What can I learn from this passage?*

Day 5: The Daughters of Jerusalem (Song of Songs 5:2—8)

As in 3:1–5, the lover searches for the loved one. Although the loved one was asleep, her heart was awake. She hears her lover knocking at her door at night, calling to her to open it for him. She teases him by appearing to reject his plea, saying she has taken off her robe which she hesitates to put on, and she washed her feet that she does not want to get dirty again. She reports her lover put his hand in through the opening, making her innermost being tremble, which appears to be a reference to her womb.

When she finally rises to open the door for him, she discovers he has gone. Deeply disappointed, she seeks him and calls out to him in vain. The watchmen, not knowing why she was out in the street, beat her and tore off her mantle. She pleads with the Daughters of Jerusalem to tell her lover, if they find him, she is sick with love.

The Daughters of Jerusalem address the woman as the most beautiful and ask how her lover differs from any other lover. The description of her lover emphasizes her loving admiration for him. He is radiant, ruddy, outstanding, with a head of gold, hair as black as a raven, eyes like doves, lips like lilies, arms like rods of gold, loins the work of ivory, legs like pillars of alabaster, and an appearance as imposing as the cedars of Lebanon.

In chapter 6, the Daughters of Jerusalem ask the beautiful woman where her lover has gone, and she answers as though she never lost him. He has come to his garden to feed and gather his lilies, an apparent reference to his erotic pleasure with his loved one.

The man speaks of the beauty of his lover like that of Tirzah, a city that was once the capital of the northern kingdom and a name that means "pleasant." She is as fair as Jerusalem. Because her eyes stir him up, he amusingly tells her to look away. To him, her hair is like a flock of goats, her teeth as white as pregnant lambs, and her cheeks like pomegranate halves. Daughters, queens, and concubines see how happy she is and praise her, viewing her as coming forth like the dawn, as beautiful as the white moon, and as pure as the blazing sun.

In chapter 7, the Daughters of Jerusalem urge her to turn and dance for them, but she refuses to be a spectacle for them. The man praises the beauty of her feet, her curving thighs, her naval, belly, breasts, her neck, her eyes, her nose, and her hair which captures the king. He compares each part of her body to some striking images such as a mound of wheat, fawns, and a tower of ivory. He continues praising her beauty and refers to her form as a date palm that he wishes to climb and her breasts like clusters on a vine. The fragrance of her breath is like apples and her mouth like the best wine.

The woman seems to interrupt, referring to the best wine as flowing down smoothly over for her lover. She belongs to her lover who, in turn, yearns for her. She invites him to go into the field and pass the night with her. Urging him to go out early to the vineyards to see if the vines are in bloom, she promises to give her love to him. She promises to share her stored-up fruits with her lover.

In chapter 8, she expresses a wish that her lover were as though her brother so they could kiss in public without anyone objecting. She would learn from him about love and give him wine to drink with his left hand under her head and his right arm embracing her. Sexual connotations are implied here.

The Daughters ask who is coming up from the desert leaning on her lover. The woman declares she awakened him under the apple tree where his mother conceived him. She praises the power of love, which she asks him to set as a seal on his heart and arm. A person's seal of love was often worn on the arm of a person. Referring to Love and Death as though each were a person no one could escape, she declares Love is as strong as Death, and longing is as fierce as Sheol. The arrows of love are arrows of fire, flames of the divine, which deep waters cannot quench. If one were to offer all his wealth for love, he would be ridiculed since love cannot be bought.

The woman speaks of brothers protecting a little sister whose breasts have not yet begun to grow. If she is as firm as a wall, she will be like a precious ornament. If she is like a door, easily opened to others, she will demand special vigilance. The woman declares she is a wall with breasts like a tower and like one who brings peace to her lover.

The man declares Solomon has a vineyard which he gave to caretakers. For its fruit, one would have to pay a thousand silver pieces. The man's vineyard is at his own disposal and he offers a thousand pieces for Solomon and 200 for the caretakers.

Her lover asks the woman for a song for others to hear, and she replies her lover is like a gazelle or a young stag on the mountains of spices.

Lectio Divina

Spend 8 to 10 minutes in silent contemplation of the following passage:

In the Song of Songs, the woman begs the one loved to set her as a seal upon his heart, meaning she identifies him as belonging to her and no one else. True love demands total commitment in the sharing of love.

✠ *What can I learn from this passage?*

Review Questions

1. What does the author of Ecclesiastes mean when he says in chapter 4:6, "Better is one handful with tranquility than two with toil and a chase after wind!"?

2. Apply Ecclesiastes 10:3 to your life: "Even when walking in the street the fool, lacking understanding, calls everyone a fool."

3. What does the Song of Songs mean when speaking of a garden in chapter 4:12?

The Book of Wisdom

But you, our God, are good and true, slow to anger, and governing all with mercy (15:1).

Opening Prayer (SEE PAGE 15)

Context

Part 1: Wisdom 1—3:12 The Book of Wisdom was written in Greek about fifty years before Christ, during a period of internal turmoil in Judea. The book shows a familiarity with earlier biblical writings and strives to enlighten and support those who remain faithful to God. Chapters 1—3:12 speak of the reward of righteousness.

Part 2: Wisdom 3:13—19 These chapters contain wisdom sayings concerning the mercy of God, false worship, and references recalling the Lord's past blessings on the Israelites.

PART 1: GROUP STUDY (WISDOM 1—3:12)

Read aloud Wisdom 1—3:12.

1—2 Immortality

The author of Wisdom exhorts rulers (kings and judges) to live righteously, sincerely seeking the Lord's goodness. Those who test the Lord separate themselves from God, demonstrating their lack of wisdom. The holy spirit of "discipline" (wisdom) is not present in those who offer senseless counsels. As kind as wisdom is, she will not release blasphemers. God, who sees all and hears all, knows the deepest thoughts of the blasphemer and will punish justly.

The author urges his readers not to choose death by their manner of life or to call down destruction on themselves by their works. When the author speaks of death, he is referring to spiritual death. Hades does not have dominion on earth. "Hades" is the Greek word for the Hebrew word "Sheol," meaning the place of the dead. Righteousness is immortal and a gift from God.

The wicked enter a covenant with death and become its friend by their words and deeds. Their allotted time on earth will pass like a shadow, and people will forget what they did while alive. No one returns from death. Because the wicked believe all ends with death, the obvious conclusion is they should enjoy themselves with wine and expensive perfumes, having no guilt when they oppress the righteous poor, the widow, and the aged.

Those who are righteous become a reproach to those who sin against the law, meaning the Law of Moses. Because the righteous profess to have knowledge of God and refer to themselves as children of God, the wicked view them as rebuking them. In return, the wicked plot to test the goodness and patience of the righteous by insulting and torturing them. They conspire to inflict a humiliating death on them to see how true their words are when they say God will take care of them.

The author views the wicked as blind, lacking knowledge of the hidden plans of God. They are unaware of the rewards of holiness and God's plan of immortality for humans. The Lord made humans in the image of God, but due to the devil's envy of human beings, spiritual death entered the world. This reference to the devil's actions recalls the temptation story in Genesis 3:1–24 and the consequences of sin. This is the first time an author connects the devil with the snake in the creation story.

3:1–12 God's Counsel Concerning Suffering

The author offers advice concerning suffering. He praises the righteous, saying their souls are in the hand of God and no torment will touch them. In the view of the foolish, their death appears to be an affliction and total destruction, but they are actually in peace. Although they appear to be punished in the eyes of the wicked, they have hope for immortality. They will suffer, not as punishment, but for cleansing, as gold is tried in a furnace. The Lord accepted them as a sacrificial offering, a reference to a burnt offering that is totally consumed.

At the time of judgment, the righteous shall shine like sparks in a fire. The faithful shall understand truth and abide with the Lord in love. The wicked, however, who rejected righteousness, will receive a punishment equal to their thoughts. Those who reject wisdom and instruction will lack hope, and their works shall be worthless. Their wives and children will be like them, foolish and cursed.

Review Questions

1. What do the early chapters of Wisdom say about immortality?
2. What does Wisdom say about a long or short life as a sign of God's love or disfavor?
3. What happens to the souls of the just?

Closing Prayer (SEE PAGE 15)

Pray the closing prayer now or after *lectio divina*.

Lectio Divina (SEE PAGE 8)

Relax your body and maintain a posture of prayer (back straight, eyes shut, feet flat on the floor). This exercise can take as long as you want, but in the context of this Bible study, 10 to 20 minutes should be sufficient.

The meditations that follow are provided only to help group participants use this prayer form, but note that *lectio* is intended to bring one to a place of prayerful contemplation where the Word of God speaks to the hearer from his or her heart. (See page 8 for further instruction.)

Immortality (1—2)

In ancient times, people did not believe in life after death. The greatest gift was to have male children to carry on one's name and to leave behind a good memory of one's life for future generations. About 150 years before the birth of Christ, the idea of resurrection slowly began to emerge. By the time Paul was writing his letters, the concept of resurrection was a major teaching of

Christianity. He writes, "For the trumpet will sound, the dead will be raised incorruptible, and we shall be changed" (1 Corinthians 15:52). The Book of Wisdom states: "For God formed us to be imperishable" (2:23).

✠ *What can I learn from this passage?*

God's Counsel Concerning Suffering (3:1–12)

Everyone in life has experienced some form of suffering. Jesus suffered. According to the author of Wisdom, people of faith who believe God is with them, even in the face of suffering and death, are in the hands of God. He tells us, "Chastised a little, they shall be greatly blessed" (3:5).

✠ *What can I learn from this passage?*

PART 2: INDIVIDUAL STUDY (WISDOM 3:13—19)

Day 1: The Judgment of the Wicked (3:13—6:21)

The barren wife who never sinned against her marriage shall bear fruit when the Lord judges souls. The faithful eunuch shall receive the reward of the faithful. The children of sinners will not be esteemed, even if they live a long life.

In chapter 4, the author states it is better to be childless and virtuous. The memory of virtue is immortal, remembered by God and human beings. Whether the children of wicked parents live a long or short life, they will live without honor and bring no comfort to their parents when God judges them. They will be witnesses of evil against their parents.

Since understanding is not measured by gray hair but by a life without sin, the righteous who die in their youth can still have possessed understanding and the fullness of many years. Some of the righteous, who lived among sinners, were taken by God lest they be lured into a sinful life. The Lord, knowing the memory of the wicked will be forgotten, will laugh at those who lack understanding and show contempt for the wise who die young.

In chapter 5, the author tells us the wicked who die will be amazed at the salvation of the righteous and realize they were fools for mocking the righteous. They became entangled in their misery, realizing they never paid attention to the way of the Lord. Looking back, they see their boasting and pride as a passing shadow, leaving no tracks behind like a ship cutting through water. Their life passes away like chaff in the wind, or fine snow, or smoke in the wind.

The righteous will live forever, protected by the Most High. Describing the Lord as though preparing for battle, the author speaks of the Lord as taking zeal for armor, righteousness for a breastplate, sure judgment for a helmet, and holiness for a shield. The universe will join with the Lord in the battle, with well-aimed lightning bolts and hailstones as though flung from a sling. The wicked will be overwhelmed by natural disasters, by churning seas, flooding rivers, and strong winds, and their evil ways will lead to their downfall.

In chapter 6, the author bids kings and judges to realize their authority comes from the Lord, who will scrutinize their works and counsels. The Lord will move quickly against those who did not judge rightly and keep the law. Since the Lord made the great as well as the poor, the Lord has the power to scrutinize the powerful. The Lord exhorts the princes to learn wisdom so they will not fall away. Those who keep the law will be holy.

Wisdom quickly makes herself known to those who desire her, and those who do so will be free from care. To observe her laws is the basis for incorruptibility and immortality, which brings one close to God. The author tells the princes they must honor Wisdom if they hope to reign forever.

Lectio Divina

Spend 8 to 10 minutes in silent contemplation of the following passage:

According to the author of the Book of Wisdom, wisdom comes to the young and the old who live with an understanding of God's law. In the Gospel of Matthew, Jesus praises the Lord of heaven and earth saying, "...although you have hidden these things from the wise and the learned you have revealed them to the childlike" (Matthew 11:25). Those who believe in God and remain faithful to God's law know more about the meaning of life than the well-educated person who does not believe in God or chooses evil over good.

✠ *What can I learn from this passage?*

Day 2: The Wisdom of Solomon (Wisdom 6:22—11:1)

The author begins to write in the first person, identifying himself with Solomon without mentioning his name. As mentioned earlier in this book, Solomon is not the author, although the book is attributed to him. In an effort to follow the author's intent, this commentary will speak as though Solomon is the true author.

Solomon intends to enlighten others with knowledge of wisdom without hiding any secrets from the reader. Since a large number of the wise brings salvation to the world and a prudent king brings stability, the author instructs the people to pay attention to his message.

In chapters 7—8:1, Solomon declares that although he is a king, he is mortal, born in the same manner as everyone else and struggling like an infant. Prudence and the spirit of Wisdom came to him as a result of his prayers. He preferred Wisdom over his position as king and viewed her as more valuable than all forms of wealth. Solomon chose Wisdom over health, beauty, and light, and he received Wisdom and all the good things coming with her.

Solomon shared the riches of Wisdom with others, knowing those who received this treasure gained the friendship of God because of her. Solomon declares his message, prudence, and knowledge are in the hand of God. Because of this, Solomon has knowledge of the universe, the hosts of heaven and their positions, yearly cycles, the natures of living things, the winds, the thoughts of human beings, the plants, and all that is hidden or clearly known.

Solomon finds in Wisdom a spirit that is intelligent, holy, unique, and possessing many other physical and spiritual attributes. Wisdom is beyond all motion and penetrates all things. She is the breath of God, a pure emanation and reflection of the glory of God. She can do all things and renews all, producing friends and prophets for God from age to age. She is more radiant than all light. While night overcomes light, wickedness never overcomes Wisdom. She is everywhere, governing mightily from one end of the world to the other.

In chapter 8:2 and the following, Solomon expresses his love for Wisdom from the time of his youth and declares his desire to take her as his bride. Even the Lord of all loved her. She teaches the greatest gifts of life, namely moderation, prudence, righteousness, and fortitude. She knows and understands all things.

Because of Wisdom, Solomon will demonstrate keen judgment before rulers who will remain silent while he speaks. Tyrannical princes will fear him. Living with Wisdom involves no bitterness and no grief but rather joy and happiness. Knowing the gifts of immortality, love, riches, prudence, and learned discourse reside with Wisdom, Solomon sought to take her as his own. Sure he could not possess Wisdom unless God granted it, Solomon prayed to God.

Chapter 9 contains Solomon's prayer. He begins by addressing God as the God of his ancestors, acknowledging the word of God created human beings to rule all creatures and to govern the world in holiness and righteousness with honest judgment. Professing himself to be a servant of the Lord, a weak human being, lacking in comprehension of judgment and laws, he begs the Lord to give him the gift of Wisdom.

Solomon recognizes the Lord instructed him to build a temple and an altar on God's holy mountain. He professes Wisdom was present with God when the Lord created the world. He begs the Lord to send Wisdom upon him so she will work with him, guiding him and teaching him what is pleasing to the Lord. With Wisdom, Solomon believes he will rule the Lord's people justly and be worthy of the throne of his father. He asks who knows God's counsel or the intentions of the Lord. The corruptible body, like an earthly tent, weighs down the mind of the people with a multitude of concerns. With Wisdom, the people learned what was pleasing to the Lord.

In chapter 10, Solomon lists how Wisdom saved the people from the beginning of the creation of humanity. Wisdom preserved the father of all (Adam), punished the one who killed his brother (Cain), saved the world from the Flood (Noah), chose a blameless man (Abraham), protected a righteous man fleeing fire cast on the five cities (Lot), established a pillar of salt as punishment for disobedience (Lot's wife), protected a righteous man who fled from his angry brother (Jacob), guarded a righteous man who was sold and locked in a dungeon (Joseph), and rescued the people from slavery (Moses), drowning the enemy.

Lectio Divina

Spend 8 to 10 minutes in silent contemplation of the following passage:

At the Last Supper, Jesus tells his disciples he will send "the Spirit of truth" to guide them in all truth (John 16:13). Many spiritual writers equate Wisdom with the Holy Spirit. Just as the Lord gave Solomon the gift of wisdom to instruct him, guide him, and protect him, so the Holy Spirit comes to us, to instruct us in all truth, guide us, and protect us.

✠ *What can I learn from this passage?*

Day 3: Providence of God During the Exodus (Wisdom 11:2—12:27)

In his prayer, Solomon speaks to the Lord concerning the Exodus experience of the Israelites. He recalls the plight of the Israelites, wandering through the wilderness where they had to battle with their enemies. When they were thirsty, the Lord gave them water from a rock. They benefited by the things that punished their foes. The prior sentence points to the examples and contrasts that follow.

The first benefit concerns water. After turning the Nile to blood in retaliation for the slaying of infants, the Lord later gave abundant, clear water to the Israelites in the desert. Before the Israelites received water in the desert, the Lord tested them by allowing them to experience extreme thirst. The Egyptians learned the Israelites benefited from the torment they had to endure. The Lord allowed the Israelites to leave Egypt on a path through water and later satisfy their thirst in the desert. As a punishment for the Egyptian worship of dumb serpents and insects, the Lord sent swarms of these dumb creatures in vengeance.

The Lord, who fashioned the universe from formless matters, could punish as the Lord wished, by sending ferocious bears, lions, and many unknown fierce-looking beasts, the mere sight of which could frighten them to death. The formless matter recalls the chaos of Genesis 1:2, before God put order into creation. The mighty Lord, however, who loves all things, has mercy on all of creation. Otherwise, how could anything have endured unless God, the ruler and lover of souls, willed it?

In chapter 12, Solomon, in his prayer, notes the Lord used the ancestors of the Israelites to destroy the sorcerers and those who sacrificed children. The Lord did not annihilate them all at once but sent wasps and an army to weaken them by degrees to afford them an opportunity to repent. Who could oppose the creator of all when the Lord decrees people are to perish, or who can argue in support of the wicked? There is no god, king, or prince who can confront God on behalf of those the Lord has punished. The Lord, who is righteous, would regard it as an unworthy use of power to punish the innocent.

As powerful as the Lord is, the Lord judges with gentleness and leniency. The Lord's actions teach the righteous they must be kind. While the Lord punishes the Israelites to correct them, the Lord scourges their enemies 10,000 times more.

The Lord punished those who strayed far like foolish children in accepting animals as gods. Those, who did not heed the Lord's mild rebukes, experienced an earned punishment from the Lord. Learning that the animals they thought were gods were unable to help them, the idolaters recognized as the true God the one they rejected. This reality brought the final condemnation upon them.

Lectio Divina

Spend 8 to 10 minutes in silent contemplation of the following passage:

> Jesus tells a story about a beggar named Lazarus, who longed to eat the scraps that fell from the table of a rich man who completely ignored him. When they both die, Lazarus is seen sharing in glory with Abraham, but the rich man is suffering a fiery torment. The rich man begs for Lazarus to dip the tip of his finger in water to cool his tongue, but Lazarus cannot cross from his side to that of the rich man's side. The rich man seeks a drop of water and must endure a torment similar to that he caused for Lazarus. The story and the prayer of Solomon intend to warn us the torment we cause for others could be a punishment we ourselves will have to endure.

✠ *What can I learn from this passage?*

Day 4: Digression on False Worship (13—15:17)

From chapter 13 to 15:17, the author digresses into a consideration of false worship. In 13:1–9, he speaks of those who examined the wonders of nature without seeing the artisan, the Creator of all. They considered fire, wind, swift air, the circuit of the stars, the mighty waters, the lights of heaven, or the governors of the world (sun and moon) as gods. They did not proceed far enough, stopping at the works of the Lord without looking to the one who created them. By studying the magnificent and powerful things of nature, they should realize how much more powerful is the one who made them.

The author assails those involved in the foolishness of idol worship. They claim products of art and images of beasts, made of useless stone, gold, or silver are gods. The carpenter cuts down a tree, scrapes off its bark, uses its scraps to prepare his food, and carves an image of a human being or some worthless beast with its refuse. He paints it with red stain to cover all its blemishes, makes for it a fitting shrine, and securely fastens it to a wall to keep it from falling. When finished, he is not ashamed to address this thing without a soul about his goods, his marriage, or his children. For power, he invokes the powerless, for life the dead, for travel something that cannot walk, and for profit he invokes powerless hands.

Chapter 14 uses the image of a fragile piece of wood (a boat) carrying a person over rough seas. The author declares it is not the piece of wood that preserves a person but God's providence that opens a way through the seas. Noah was without skill, yet the Lord guided him safely over the seas on a raft. The use of the word "raft" stresses the fragile nature of Noah's ship. The author refers to the period as a time when the proud giants were being destroyed. This is a reference to the Nephilim whom the people of Noah's day considered to be giants (see Genesis 6:4). Guided by the Lord, Noah's safe journey provided a future for the human family.

The evildoer who made the idol and worships it is as despicable to the Lord as the thing itself. They will both be punished. Because the idols of the nations laid alluring snares for the human soul, they shall also be cursed.

Human emptiness leads to the invention of idols. A mourning father makes an image of a deceased child who is then honored as a god and hands it on until it becomes observed as a law. Kings became worshiped by royal decree. As a result, those at a distance copied the image of the king to flatter the absent one as though present. Artisans skillfully carved even more beautiful images of the king, leading the people to worship these as gods. Such idols became traps for them.

The author not only laments the people's ignorance about God but also the results of their ignorance, which are child sacrifice and hysterical exotic rituals that lead to adultery. Their confusion leads them to commit murder, theft, corruption, infidelity, chaos, deceitfulness, harassment of the good, forgetfulness of gratitude, lust, and adultery. Because they rejected God by serving idols and deliberately swore false oaths, they will be punished, not by the idols they worshiped, but by the just reckoning for their wicked deeds.

In chapter 15, the author praises the goodness of the Lord, who is slow to anger and governs all with mercy. He believes righteous people will recognize the power of God as the reason for their immortality and will not deviate from the worship of God.

The potter makes vessels out of clay and from the same clay makes idols. Although he was formed from the clay of the earth and shall return to clay after his death, the potter is the one who gives each one its meaning. He competes with goldsmiths, silversmiths, and molders of bronze in fashioning idols. Because he makes idols without knowing the one who fashioned him and breathed life into him, his heart is more worthless than the earth he uses. He is aware his images are merely fragile images of clay made for a profit.

The enemies who believed the idols of their nation would protect them and bring them victory are the most stupid of all. The idols cannot see, breathe, hear, touch, or walk. The enemies, mere human beings, are mortal and depend for breath on God, who made them.

Lectio Divina

Spend 8 to 10 minutes in silent contemplation of the following passage:

Idols can be like those condemned in the Book of Wisdom, mere images without life, or they can be idols of our own making, driving us to greed, jealousy, power, or other forms of selfishness. Jesus said, "Much will be required of the person entrusted with much, and still more will be demanded of the person entrusted with more" (Luke 12:48). Much is required of a person with good health, intelligence, wealth, exceptional skills, or some other gift from God. When our gifts enhance only ourselves or make us proud or sinful, they become our idols, taking the place of God in our life. God's gifts are given for the common good.

✠ *What can I learn from this passage?*

Day 5: Punishment and Blessings (15:18—19:22)

God punishes the Egyptians and protects the Israelites. The Egyptians showed how loathsome they were in worshiping unsightly beasts and they perished by similar creatures, a swarm of insects (see Exodus 10:1–20). While the swarm of insects in everything in Egypt made the Egyptians lose their appetite for all kinds of food, the Lord provided quail in the desert for the Israelites after a short period of deprivation (see Exodus 16:4–15).

When the Israelites in the desert complained against God and Moses, God sent small serpents whose poisonous bite killed many of the people. When the Israelites admitted their sinfulness, Moses mounted an image of a bronze serpent on a pole, and whenever a serpent bit someone, the individual would look at the bronze serpent and recover (see Numbers 21:4–9). The author of Wisdom recognizes it was not the bronze serpent the people looked at that saved them, but it was the Lord who healed them.

Another contrast concerned hail and lightning sent upon the Egyptians. When Pharaoh refused to allow the Israelites to leave Egypt, the Lord sent lightning and hail upon them (see Exodus 9:22–26). The Israelites, however, received manna from heaven, which the author of Wisdom refers to in 16:20 as "food of angels" (see Exodus 16:4–9). The miraculous aspect of the manna was that it could be baked in an oven but would melt under the power of the sun. The Israelites were to instruct their children it was the Word of God and not the different kinds of food that sustained the people.

In chapter 17, the author elaborates on the ninth plague, darkness sent upon Egypt by the Lord (see Exodus 10:21–23). The darkness terrified the Egyptians, who could not overcome the darkness even with the light of a fire. Some intermittent flashes of light, most likely referring to lightning, caused greater fear than if they did not take place. The sound of insects and reptiles terrified them. Their torment came from not knowing what caused the darkness. Every noise frightened the Egyptians, whether it was whistling wind, songs of birds, rushing water, falling rocks, the gallop of animals, the cry of fierce beasts, or a sound from the hollow of the hills. Except for Egypt, the world shone with brightness and people continued their daily work. The thoughts of the Egyptians became a greater burden to them than was the darkness.

Chapter 18 speaks of the holy ones (the Israelites) being led by a great light. The Book of Exodus speaks of a column of cloud leading the Israelites during the day and a column of fire to lead them at night (see Exodus 13:21). The author of Wisdom states the Egyptians, although they could not see the Israelites, could hear them, leading them to thank the Israelites for not harming them.

The Pharaoh in Egypt ordered all the firstborn of the Israelites to be drowned in the Nile River. Moses was saved when the Pharaoh's daughter found him floating in a basket, and she raised him in her court (see Exodus 1:12—2:10). The author of Wisdom views the Lord as retaliating by drowning a multitude of the Egyptians in the Nile.

In his prayer, the author speaks of the death of the firstborn of every Egyptian. The Israelites, knowing in advance the Lord would act against the Egyptians, offered a sacrifice in secret and prayed the divine institution together. The divine institution refers to the Passover. The whole of Egypt mourned over the death of so many of their inhabitants, and they could not bury them all. The Egyptians had to acknowledge the Israelites were the people of God.

In the desert, a plague afflicted the Israelites, but the Lord's wrath did not last long. Although 14,700 people died, Aaron went among the people with the censor, and the remaining members of the community were cured of the plague (see Numbers 17:11–15). He was a blameless man whose weapon was a censor and who hastened to be their champion. The power of God saved them, not by bodily strength, but by the Word of the Lord. The world was inscribed on his priestly garment, and the glories of the ancestors were engraved on four rows of stones on the garment. There was a diadem on his head.

In chapter 19, the author asserts God knew in advance the Egyptians would quickly send the Israelites away from their land and would change their mind and pursue them. The Egyptians reached a foolish decision in their mourning, pursued the Israelites, and drowned in the Nile, completing their punishment. The Israelite nation passed through the dry and grassy plains of the Red Sea, praising the Lord who delivered them. The Lord's gift of quail came up to them from the sea.

The people of Egypt practiced hatred toward strangers, while others simply refused to receive strangers in their midst. The Egyptians made slaves of the guests who were their benefactors, a reference to the Israelites who came into Egypt centuries earlier.

Those who received strangers with hostility will receive some sort of punishment, while those who received them with festive celebrations and afterward afflicted them with terrible suffering were stricken with blindness. This refers to the story of Lot. When the people of his hometown wanted to have their way with two of his visitors who were angels, the angels struck them blind so they could not find the door (see Genesis 19:1–11).

The author refers to land animals transformed into water creatures, which seems to refer to the Israelites passing through the Red Sea. In referring to creatures that swim and move over the land, he is apparently speaking of the frogs invading Egypt. Fire, as in the story of Daniel in the fiery furnace, did not consume the perishable animals that walked among them, nor did it melt the manna. In everything, the Lord exalted and glorified the Israelites, helping them at all times and in all places.

Lectio Divina

Spend 8 to 10 minutes in silent contemplation of the following passage:

Memories from the past inspired the Israelites to remain faithful in the present. Wisdom consists in remembering the blessings of the Lord in the past and trusting that God is still acting to protect and guide the people in the present. Christians recall the life and message of Jesus and apply the message of his life to the present. For Jews and Christians, their past heritage leads to their present glory.

✠ *What can I learn from this passage?*

Review Questions

1. Why does the author of Wisdom believe living a righteous life to be necessary for immortality?
2. Why does the author attribute the Book of Wisdom to Solomon?
3. What does the history of the Israelites teach the Israelites?

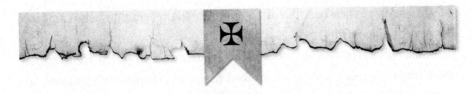

The Book of Sirach

THE WISDOM OF BEN SIRA (ECCLESIASTICUS)

The root of wisdom is to fear the Lord; her branches are long life (1:20).

Opening Prayer (SEE PAGE 15)

Context

Part 1: Sirach (1—4) At the end of the Wisdom of Ben Sira (Sirach), we learn the name of the author is "Yeshua Ben Eleazar Ben Sira," which means "Jesus, Son of Eleazar, Son of Sira." The name "Sirach" comes from the author's name in Greek.

Ben Sira possessed a love for the wisdom tradition, the law, priesthood, Temple, and divine worship, as will become evident in studying this book. The book stresses obedience to parents, relationships with neighbors, and concern for the poor and needy.

Sirach dates to the early second century before Christ and was translated from Hebrew into Greek after 117 BC by a grandson of Ben Sira. The grandson appended a foreword to the book stating he was translating and publishing it for those wanting to live their lives according to the law.

Part 2: Sirach 5—51 The Wisdom of Ben Sira (Sirach) continues with moral instructions, a eulogy for the heroes of Israel, and two appendixes. The author lists a number of proverbs, one after the other.

PART 1: GROUP STUDY (SIRACH 1—4)

Read aloud Sirach 1—4.

1—2 God's Gift of Wisdom

All wisdom comes from the Lord in whom it resides forever. Wisdom knows all: the sands, drops of rain, heaven's height, the extent of the earth, the abyss, and wisdom itself. She was created before all else by the Lord, she filled every work of the Lord, and she lavished on those who love the Lord.

As in previous books of Wisdom, the author exalts fear of the Lord as the festive crown of the Lord. Those who practice fear of the Lord are those who practice true religion by loving and serving God and keeping the law. It is total reverence for God. Fear of the Lord brings the blessings of a long life and joy, even on the day of one's death. The beginning of wisdom is the fear of the Lord. It drives away sin, helps a person avoid unjust anger, and conveys patience. The way to wisdom is to keep the Lord's commandments. Wisdom avoids hypocrisy and boasting. Because the humble and deceitful do not practice fear of the Lord, the Lord will shame them in the assembly (community Temple worship).

In chapter 2, Ben Sira warns the just to expect trials in life and to live with a sincere heart, avoiding all rash actions and impatience in time of misfortune. As evidenced by those who trusted God in the past, those who fear the Lord should live with trust so they will not lose their reward. The Lord acts with compassion and mercy, forgiving sins and protecting people in peril. Those who fear the Lord, love the Lord and keep the Lord's commands. Ben Sira bids the people to place themselves in the hands of the merciful Lord and not in the hands of mortals.

3—4 Responsibilities Before the Lord

Ben Sira views parents as holding their high position in the family due to the will of the Lord. Those who honor their father will atone for sins, will have joy in their own children, will have their prayers answered, will live a long life. Those who obey the Lord honor their mother and serve their parents as their masters. A father's blessing provides firm roots; a mother's curse destroys the root. A father's disgrace brings no glory to children, but the father's glory brings credit to the children. Even if the father's mind should fail, children must care for him. Kindness to a father will take lasting root and provide help in time of trouble. Those who neglect their father are blasphemers, and those who provoke their mother are cursed by the Creator.

Ben Sira speaks to his son, advising him to be humble. He should not seek goals out of reach or hidden, giving himself totally to a realistic commitment. Conceit is rampant among human beings and has led many astray. In the end, a stubborn and proud heart will have many pains, with no hope of being cured. Almsgiving atones for sins. Kindness never fails.

In chapter 4:1–10, Ben Sira urges his child not to neglect the poor who look to him for help and not to delay helping the hungry, the needy, or the beggar. The Lord will be merciful to the one who listens to the needs of the poor and the orphan.

In 4:11, Wisdom begins to speak. Those who love Wisdom will be tested and, if they pass the test, they will be led to the right path. The faithful and their descendants will possess Wisdom. Those who abandon Wisdom will be abandoned.

In 4:20, the father again begins to speak. He advises his son to remain alert for the right time, fearing evil, showing no favoritism, sharing knowledge at the proper time, and always speaking the truth. He is not to bow down to a fool but before rulers. If he fights for right, even to death, the Lord will battle for him. The father tells his son not to be proud or lazy or suspicious of his servants, and to open his hand when it is time to give.

Review Questions

1. Why do Wisdom writers believe fear of the Lord is necessary for wisdom?
2. What does Ben Sira say about trusting God?
3. How does care for one's parents help the child?

Closing Prayer (SEE PAGE 15)

Pray the closing prayer now or after *lectio divina*.

Lectio Divina (SEE PAGE 8)

Relax your body and maintain a posture of prayer (back straight, eyes shut, feet flat on the floor). This exercise can take as long as you want, but in the context of this Bible study, 10 to 20 minutes should be sufficient.

The meditations that follow are provided only to help group participants use this prayer form, but note that *lectio* is intended to bring one to a place of prayerful contemplation where the Word of God speaks to the hearer from his or her heart. (See page 8 for further instruction.)

God's Gift of Wisdom (1—2)

Just as the other authors of the Wisdom Books point to fear of the Lord as the beginning of wisdom, Ben Sira does the same. The person who meditates on the Lord with reverence and awe and who trusts the Lord will live a life of justice and peace.

✠ *What can I learn from this passage?*

Responsibilities Before the Lord (3—4)

To the Israelites, respect and care for parents are the highest virtues they can perform. The father in Sirach speaks of the rewards for those who honor their parents. Concern for parents is still a major obligation for living a faithful Christian life.

✠ *What can I learn from this passage?*

PART 2: INDIVIDUAL STUDY (SIRACH 5—51)

Day 1: The Blessings of Wisdom (5—13)

Chapter 5 addresses the vices of the rich, warning them not to rely on their wealth, believing themselves to be so powerful not even the Lord can prevail over them. They presume the Lord will act with mercy, despite their many sins. Ben Sira tells the pompous rich they should turn to the Lord lest the Lord take vengeance on them and they perish.

People should be firm and consistent in what they know, paying attention, replying slowly, and remaining silent when they have nothing true to share.

Ben Sira warns against being deceitful and slandering a neighbor.

In chapter 6, Ben Sira warns against being overcome by passion that will consume a person's strength and make him a mockery for his enemies. He says agreeable speech increases the number of friends. A person may have many friends, but one in a thousand is a confidant. Faithful friends are a real treasure beyond price. Those who fear the Lord will find such friends and enjoy a stable friendship.

Ben Sira speaks of discipline that brings wisdom from youth to old age. Instead of being a burden, all her restraints will be like a splendid crown. He urges his readers to reflect on the commandments. If they do so, the Most High will make them as wise as they desire.

In chapter 7, Ben Sira tells his children they should not seek authority or places of honor by flaunting their good deeds and wisdom before the Lord or rulers, nor should they seek to become a judge if they are too weak to punish crime. They should not neglect almsgiving, should not ridicule, plot evil against a relative or friend, tell lies, speak too much in the presence of the elders, avoid hard work, or look down on others.

Ben Sira advises love of servants, care for livestock, correction of children, provision of a sensible husband for one's daughter, good treatment for one's wife, and honor for one's parents. He also exhorts fearing God, respecting priests, providing for the poor, honoring the dead, mourning with those who mourn, visiting the sick, and keeping in mind one's last days to help one to avoid sin.

In chapter 8, Ben Sira directs his children not to contend with the mighty, quarrel with the rich or loud mouths, reproach one who repents, insult someone who is old, neglect to listen to the lessons of the wise, give collateral beyond their means, join with the ruthless, or reveal their heart to anyone.

In chapter 9, Ben Sira offers wisdom concerning the attitude of his learners toward women. They should not allow a woman to destroy the learner's dignity, nor entertain evil thoughts about a virgin, nor give themselves to a prostitute, nor recline at table with a married woman.

Ben Sira declares a new friend can be like new wine that can age and become better. To avoid the fear of death, the learners should avoid those who can kill, associate with the wise, and speak with them about the Most High.

In chapter 10, Ben Sira states God is sovereign over the earth and makes proper appointments at the right time. Fear of the Lord brings honor to human beings. The prince, ruler, and judge are held in honor, but they are not honored more than those who fear God. The poor and wealthy alike can be honored for their wisdom, but they can both be disgraced if they lack fear of the Lord.

In chapter 11, Ben Sira warns against mocking those who have only loin cloths to wear or are experiencing affliction. In the Lord's hidden design, many of the oppressed are surprisingly raised to the throne, while many of the exalted fall in disgrace. Good and evil, life and death, poverty and riches are all from the Lord. At the time of death, the Lord repays mortals according to their deeds.

In chapter 12, Ben Sira teaches doing good for the evil person has no reward, so it should be avoided. It is difficult to know one's friends in prosperity, while an enemy will not remain hidden in adversity. People should never trust their enemies, even if they appear to be friendly.

In chapter 13, Ben Sira declares the rich boast of their wicked deeds, use the poor when they need them, and ignore them when they do not. People listen to the rich when they speak, even when they speak like a fool. When the poor speak wisdom, no one listens.

Day 2: God's Wisdom in Creation (14—22)

In chapter 14, Ben Sira praises those who hurt no one and have a clear conscience. The wealthy, however, have foolish worries. When the foolish miser dies, a stranger takes possession of his wealth.

In chapter 15, Ben Sira declares Wisdom will support those seeking her like a mother or a young bride, rewarding them with the bread of learning and the water of understanding. Ben Sira teaches God created human beings with the ability to choose or not to choose their behavior. The Wisdom of God sees all, never commanding anyone to sin and never showing leniency to sinners.

In chapter 16, Ben Sira states one child who is just is worth more than a thousand who are wicked. He states the Wisdom of God has allotted to every created thing and every person his or her task.

In chapter 17, Ben Sira states human beings have an allotted number of days. The Lord created them in the image and likeness of their Creator, filled them with knowledge and understanding, gave them authority over everything on earth, instructed them about good and evil, taught them to praise the name of the Lord, made an everlasting covenant with them, and revealed the commandments to them.

In chapter 18, Ben Sira teaches no one can fathom the depth of the works, the power, and the mercy of God. If human beings live to the amazing age of a hundred, the years are still "like a drop of water from the sea" or a grain of sand compared to eternity. Ben Sira notes a harsh word can spoil a good gift, and he urges the people to offer a kind word with the gift.

In chapter 19, Ben Sira continues to warn against excessive indulgence with wine, women, and prostitutes, warning his children these excesses will strip them of all they have.

Instead of acting like a fool in spreading gossip, people should question others about whom they heard some gossip before accusing them. These others may be innocent of the false gossip, or, if the gossip is true, that person may not do it again. It is better to have little understanding and fear the Lord than to have great intelligence and violate the Law.

In chapter 20, Ben Sira speaks of the value of silence and speech at the proper time. The wise remains silent until the right time comes, while a boasting fool is unaware of the proper time. Gifts from fools will do those who receive them no good, for the fool will lend today and ask for them tomorrow. A lie is continually on the lips of the fool. The wise advance themselves by their words and actions.

In chapter 21, Ben Sira states the prayer of the poor goes from the lips of the poor to God, who answers quickly. Sinners hate reproof while those who revere the Lord repent. The knowledge of the wise will increase like a life-giving stream, but the mind of a fool is like a broken jar that holds no knowledge. When those who are intelligent hear a wise word, they praise it and add to it, but a fool laughs at it and throws it away.

In chapter 22, Ben Sira states idlers are like a filthy stone or dung that they shake from their hand. A sensible daughter finds her own husband. Whoever tells a story to a fool is telling a story to someone who is drowsing. The mind of the wise is like a wooden beam that will not be destroyed by an earthquake, whereas a timid mind will not remain firm against any fear. Insulting a friend, disclosing a friend's secret, or abusing a friend will make a friend flee.

Lectio Divina

Spend 8 to 10 minutes in silent contemplation of the following passage:

> The Wisdom of Ben Sira comes down to living a good life, trusting the Lord, and remaining firm against all temptations. Among Ben Sira's many proverbs is an image of a firm beam that will not be destroyed by an earthquake. Fear of the Lord is not only the beginning of wisdom, but it is also the foundation for living as a faithful servant of the Lord.

✠ *What can I learn from this passage?*

Day 3: Praise and Warnings Concerning Wisdom (23—31)

Ben Sira addresses God as "Lord, Father and Master of my life" to express his personal relationship with God. He pleads with the Lord to protect him from becoming proud, a glutton, or lustful. Ben Sira warns his children to avoid the constant use of oaths. They are guilty if they swear in error, or if they swear and do not fulfill their promise, or if they swear for no reason helping them at all times and in all places. At all. Such swearing is not heard from the pious. The man who dishonors his marriage bed refuses to believe the Most High can see him. It will be the same for a woman who has born a child not belonging to her husband. She and her children down to the tenth generation will be excluded from the assembly of the Lord (see Deuteronomy 23:3).

In chapter 24, Wisdom speaks in the first person, declaring she came from the mouth of the Most High "and covered the earth like a mist" (24:3). Wisdom took root in Jerusalem, the city the Most High loved, where she flourished like majestic forests and stretched out her branches to all who desired wisdom. Those who eat and drink of wisdom will hunger and thirst for more. At the end of the chapter, Ben Sira interjects, mentioning his teachings on wisdom and calling them "instruction like prophecy" (24:33).

In chapter 25, Wisdom expresses delight in harmony among relatives, friendship among neighbors, and a wife and husband living happily together. Wisdom hates a proud pauper, a rich liar, and a lustful old fool. Ben Sira speaks of the sufferings of husbands married to wicked women, saying there is no venom greater than that of a wicked woman.

In chapter 26, Ben Sira speaks of the blessings a good wife bestows on her husband, bringing a smile to his face. A wife jealous of another wife is misery, making others feel the lash of her tongue. The good wife puts flesh on the bones of her husband, shows self discipline, is modest, cares for a well-ordered home, possesses a beautiful face, and presents a stately figure.

In chapter 27, Ben Sira cautions about the use of speech, saying the assessment of people is in their conversation. Conversation with the godly always brings wisdom, while conversation with fools changes like the moon. The wrangling of proud fools leads to bloodshed, and it is painful to hear their cursing. Whoever betrays a secret will do hopeless damage and never find a congenial friend.

In chapter 28, Ben Sira tells the children they will have their sins forgiven if they forgive the wrong a neighbor did to them. They should remember the covenant made with the Most High and overlook faults. Ben Sira speaks of the ravages wrought by a malicious tongue, saying it destroys strong cities and overthrows houses of the great. Sheol is preferred to the death inflicted by an evil tongue.

In chapter 29, Ben Sira speaks about lending. People keep the commandments by lending to their neighbor, but many borrowers cause trouble for those who help them. At the time of payment, the borrower delays, makes excuses, pays only half, or pays with curses and insults. Ben Sira urges his children to be patient with those in humble circumstances and to follow the commandments by helping the poor in their need. He notes people's needs are water, bread, and clothing. The life of the poor under their own roof is better than sumptuous banquets among strangers. Whether people have little or much, they should be content with what they have.

In chapter 30, Ben Sira advocates chastising a son often to discipline him so he may give joy to his parents when he grows up. When the father dies, he will not seem to be dead since he leaves behind someone like himself. The pampered, untrained son will bring terror upon the family when he grows up. Ben Sira adds a note about good health, saying it is better to be poor with vigorous health than to be rich with physical ills. Those who are cheerful and merry at table benefit from the food they eat.

In chapter 31, Ben Sira speaks of the anxiety experienced by the rich who have difficulty sleeping. They work to pile up wealth and, if they rest, it is to enjoy pleasure. The poor labor for a paltry living, and if they rest, they become needy. Blessed is the rich person who is found without fault. The children are to eat what is set before them without gorging themselves. People bless those who are generous with food. Ben Sira praises wine as bringing joy to the heart and warns against drinking too much.

Lectio Divina

Spend 8 to 10 minutes in silent contemplation of the following passage:

> The Wisdom of Ben Sira (Sirach) tells us to be content with what we have and to share our gifts with others in need. It is not how much we have that matters; it is how we use what we have that matters.

✠ *What can I learn from this passage?*

Day 4: Trust in the Lord and Not in Dreams (32—41)

Ben Sira continues to speak of etiquette. He warns those chosen to preside at a dinner not to be puffed up, but to be one with the guests and share in their joy. Those who are older have a right to speak, but they should speak at the correct time. The young should speak only when necessary, but they should be brief. All should leave in good time and not be the last to go home. Above all, they should bless their Maker. Those who keep the law protect themselves, and whoever trusts in the Lord will not experience shame.

In chapter 33, Ben Sira says no evil can harm those who fear the Lord, no matter what they must endure. Prudent people trust in the Word of the Lord. The fool lacks this trust. The Lord shaped the good and the wicked out of clay, exalting those who trust and bringing down those who do not trust. Ben Sira says he labored, not only for himself but also for those he wished to instruct. Masters should make a slave work so he will need rest, but not allow him to be idle or he will want to be free. If they have even one slave, they should treat him as they would like to be treated.

In chapter 34, Ben Sira warns about dreams, saying they led many people astray unless they came as an intervention from the Most High. He praises those who fear the Lord, saying the eyes of the Lord are on those who trust the Lord. The Lord is not pleased with gifts and sacrificial offerings from the godless. Who will hear the prayer of those who fast for sins and then go and commit the sins again?

In chapter 35, Ben Sira says the sacrifice of the just is accepted and never

---

forgotten by the Lord. Those who give to the Most High as the Most High has given to them will find a reward from the Lord. Gifts gained through extortion are not acceptable to the Lord, a God of justice. The cry of the poor pierces the clouds and will not leave till the Most High responds and destroys the power of the wicked and repays the good with justice.

In chapter 36, Ben Sira prays for God's people, begging God to raise a hand against foreign nations so they may see the Lord's mighty deeds. The salvation of the Israelites showed the glory of the Lord to other nations, and Ben Sira now prays that the Lord will use the weakness of the nations before Israel to show the glory of the Lord. Ben Sira also seeks to explain the importance of discernment in choosing associates, such as a wife.

In chapter 37, Ben Sira speaks of the blessings and dangers of friendship. Some are friends in name only, while good friends will fight with them against the enemy. A friend who becomes an enemy brings sorrow. Ben Sira urges the children to associate with religious people who are like-minded. They should trust their heart and pray to the Lord to set them on the right path.

Ben Sira stresses the power of words in public speech. Some may be wise and benefit many, yet appear to themselves to be foolish. Those who are wise and accept it find full enjoyment and win a heritage of glory. Ben Sira warns against gluttony, which leads to sickness.

In chapter 38, Ben Sira urges those he is instructing to make use of doctors whom God has established in their profession. He praises the work of the doctors and the healing herbs produced by the earth by which the doctors heal and ease pain. Since God is the one who heals, Ben Sira urges his students to pray when they are ill and to avoid evil. The doctor also prays to God.

Ben Sira urges mourning for the dead, but once they are carried away, all mourning should end, since there is no hope for them to return from the grave. The scribe, the one who plows, the engraver and designer, the smith, and the potter work on the daily maintenance of life.

In chapter 39, Ben Sira speaks of those who devote themselves to study of the law of the Most High, exploring the wisdom of the ancients. They safeguard the discourses of the famous, search for the hidden meaning of proverbs, journey to distant lands, and rise early. Ben Sira urges his children to praise the works of the Lord. All the works of the Lord are good, and they supply for every need, each having its own worth at the proper time.

In chapter 40, Ben Sira speaks of the joys and miseries of life. The Lord has placed a heavy yoke on all human beings, whether king or commoner, who live with troubled thoughts and fear of heart, even at night while they attempt to rest. Plague, bloodshed, heat, drought, plunder, famine, and death are all part of life. A devoted wife is better than cattle or orchards, and love of friends is better than wine and strong drink. No matter how wonderful the gifts of creation are, fear of the Lord provides an abundance of blessings.

In chapter 41, Ben Sira teaches that death comes to everyone: to the successful and the serene, the weak, the elderly, and the children of sinners. This is in accord with God's law. A virtuous name will never be forgotten.

Ben Sira speaks of reasons for true shame. Children should be ashamed of immorality before their father and mother, falsehood before prince and ruler, deceit before master and mistress, and disloyalty before an associate and friend. All should be ashamed of sinful deeds.

Lectio Divina

Spend 8 to 10 minutes of silent contemplation of the following passage:

> Many people live openly sinful lives without showing any shame for their sinfulness. In some cases, sinfulness is praised and the sinful become popular for being brave enough to openly declare their opposition to the laws of God. Great nations have floundered and collapsed when their morals collapsed. The lack of shame in a nation allowing sin can lead to disaster.

✠ *What can we learn from this passage?*

Day 5: Remembering Their Ancestors (42—51)

In chapter 42, Ben Sira identifies those actions which are shameful, such as betraying a secret, but there are some things that are not shameful, such as remaining faithful to the Law of the Most High. Ben Sira lists those things which are not sinful which should be mentioned, including sharing expenses, dividing an inheritance, the accuracy of scales, the constant training of children, or a number of other similar virtues.

Ben Sira continues to show his mistrust of women as he speaks of the need for a father to protect the virginity of his daughter, assuring she will be well prepared for a just marriage. He believes it is better to have a frightened daughter than a family in disgrace.

Ben Sira speaks of the works of God that were brought into being by the Word of the Lord. Just as the shining sun is seen by all, so the glory of the Lord fills all the works of the Lord. They differ one from the other, yet none of them has God created in vain. Each is good.

In chapter 43, Ben Sira continues to speak of the wonders of creation created by the Lord, from the firmament to the earth, each with its own reason for being created. After speaking of the wonders of creation, Ben Sira notes God deserves our praise since we cannot fathom the depths of the Lord. The Lord is greater than all the works in creation.

In chapter 44, Ben Sira praises Israel's ancestors, those who received great glory from the Lord. These included rulers, counselors, princes, lawgivers, sages, composers of psalms, and others whose names are forgotten. All were godly whose good deeds were not forgotten and their good deeds continue in the lives of their descendants. They are buried in peace and their name lives on. Ben Sira names some of these people who glorified the Lord: Noah, Abraham, Isaac, and Israel (Jacob).

In chapter 45, Ben Sira lists the great people of the Israelites. When Moses spoke, God performed great signs and delivered the commandments to him. The Lord chose Aaron from the tribe of Levi and bestowed on him the office of priesthood, clothing him in splendid vestments, which Ben Sira describes at length. Moses ordained Aaron, anointing him with holy oil. He was chosen to bless the people in the name of the Lord and sacrifice burnt offerings to the Lord on behalf of the people. When the followers of Dathan, Abiram, and the band of Korah rebelled against Moses and Aaron, the Lord destroyed them (see Numbers 16).

The family of Aaron did not receive a portion of land as the other tribes of Israel did, but they served all the tribes and were supported by the offerings of the people. Phinehas, the son of Eleazar and grandson of Aaron, killed an Israelite and a pagan woman for the sake of the community and alleviated the Lord's anger concerning idol worship (see Numbers 25:6–15). The Lord bestowed the high priesthood on him and his descendants. The Lord chose David and his son, but the priesthood was forever.

In chapter 46, Ben Sira continues to extol the ancestors of the Israelites, naming Joshua as the valiant warrior who led the people into the Promised Land along with his companion, Caleb. They were the only two survivors among those who escaped from Egypt under the leadership of Moses. Ben Sira blesses the memory of the judges who did not abandon God. Naming Samuel as a judge who offered sacrifice, Ben Sira declares the Lord chose Samuel for a prophetic office. He established the kingdom, anointed kings, and became a sought-after guide for the Israelites.

In chapter 47, Ben Sira speaks of Nathan, David, and Solomon. Nathan, the prophet, served David, who defeated the Philistines and received the royal crown. Due to David's merits, Solomon, a wise son, succeeded him and built the Temple. He astounded others with his wisdom. Because of his sins, however, his kingdom was divided in two after his death. The southern kingdom (Judah) was ruled by Solomon's son, and the northern kingdom (Israel, also referred to as Ephraim) was ruled by Jeroboam, a servant of Solomon who rebelled against the king.

In chapter 48, Ben Sira speaks of Elijah, the prophet who brought fire down from heaven, raised a dead body to life, sent kings to their destruction, and was taken up in a chariot with fiery horses, and who is destined to return before the day of the Lord. Elisha was filled with the spirit of Elijah and performed twice as many marvels. Despite the wonders and deeds of Elisha, the people did not repent. King Hezekiah of Judah built a conduit to bring water into Jerusalem. King Sennacherib of Assyria invaded Judah, and the Lord saved the people of Judah because of their prayers for help and the prophetic acts of Isaiah.

In chapter 49, Ben Sira speaks of Josiah and the prophets. King Josiah followed the Lord of Israel and destroyed the idols in the land. Since all the kings of Judah were evil except David, Hezekiah, and Josiah, the Lord turned the land over to foreign nations, as foretold by Jeremiah, who was mistreated. The prophet Ezekiel received a vision and described the different creatures of the chariot (see Ezekiel 1:4–21). He also referred to Job, who remained faithful (see Ezekiel 14:14, 20) and to the twelve minor prophets. Ben Sira speaks of Zerubbabel, Jeshua, and Nehemiah, who rebuilt the altar and Temple in Jerusalem. Among those he extols is Joseph, the son of Jacob, who brought the family of Israel into Egypt.

In chapter 50, Ben Sira, who was a contemporary of Simeon the high priest, states during Simeon's time (219–196 BC) the Temple was renovated, a reservoir was dug, and the city was fortified against the enemy. Showering him with praise for his noble deeds, Ben Sira describes him as resplendent in his glorious robes and vestments and majestically leading the sons of Aaron (the priests) and people in adoration of the Most High God and in bestowing the Lord's blessings on the people. In an epilogue, Ben Sira ends the chapter in a fashion unique among the biblical writers by identifying himself as "Yeshua Ben Eleazar Ben Sira." He states that readers who follow his message will be able to cope with anything. The fear of the Lord will be their lamp. This epilogue appears to be the original end of the book.

In chapter 51, Ben Sira prayerfully thanks the Lord for preserving him from slander, from his foes, from those who wished to kill him. When he was on the brink of death and had no one to help him, he remembered to call on the Lord for help, and the Lord answered his prayer. For this he thanks and praises the Lord. From his youth, he sought and received wisdom. He gratefully praises his teacher (Wisdom), who instructed him. He resolved to seek her, became preoccupied with her, and gradually came to know her secrets. Inviting his students to learn from him, he urges them to gain wisdom for themselves at no cost. If they work hard at learning wisdom, God will grant them their reward.

Lectio Divina

Spend 8 to 10 minutes in silent contemplation of the following passage:

> The proof of the value of Wisdom for Ben Sira is the memory of the ancestors of the Israelites who remained faithful to the Lord and performed great deeds for the nation. He longs to pass this example of wisdom, faithfulness, and courage on to his students. For him, fear of the Lord, which is the practice of awe and reverence in the presence of the Lord, is the beginning and purpose of Wisdom.

✠ *What can I learn from this passage?*

Review Questions

1. What are your thoughts about the blessings of Wisdom found in chapter 6?

2. What are your thoughts about moderation and patience found in chapter 11?

3. What are some modern applications of true and false shame found in chapter 41:14–22?

About the Author

William A. Anderson, DMin, PhD, is a presbyter of the Diocese
of Wheeling-Charleston, West Virginia. A director of retreats and
parish missions, professor, catechist, spiritual director, and a former
pastor, he has written extensively on pastoral, spiritual, and religious
subjects. Father Anderson earned his doctor of ministry degree from
St. Mary's Seminary & University in Baltimore, and his doctorate in
sacred theology from Duquesne University in Pittsburgh.

CPSIA information can be obtained
at www.ICGtesting.com
Printed in the USA
LVOW01s0254260417
532195LV00031B/1853/P